Entrée to Asia

A Culinary Adventure with Thomas Robson

Additional text by Randolph Eustace-Walden

RAINCOAST BOOKS

Vancouver

First published in 1999 by

Raincoast Books
8680 Cambie Street
Vancouver, B.C.
V6P 6M9
(604) 323-7100

www.raincoast.com

1 2 3 4 5 6 7 8 9 10

CANADIAN CATALOGUING IN PUBLICATION DATA

Robson, Thomas, 1964-
Entrée To Asia

Includes index.
ISBN 1-55192-202-9

1. Robson, Thomas, 1964- –Journeys–Asia, Southeastern. 2. Cookery, Southeast Asian. I. Title
TX724.5.S68R62 1999   641.5959   C99-910493-4

Printed in Canada

Editing by Ruth Wilson
Design by Ben Blackstock
Recipe food styling by Stephen Wong
Food Photography by Kevin Miller
Dishes for recipe shots courtesy of Ming Wo, Vancouver

Le Conseil des Arts | The Canada Council
DU CANADA | FOR THE ARTS
DEPUIS 1957 | SINCE 1957

*Raincoast Books gratefully acknowledges the support of the Government of Canada,
through the Book Publishing Industry Development Program, the Canada Council and
the Department of Canadian Heritage. We also acknowledge the assistance of the Province of British Columbia,
through the British Columbia Arts Council.*

Do you like Chinese food? Thai food perhaps? What about some of the more exotic dishes from Singapore or Malaysia?

What if I told you I could take you out of your kitchen and travel all over Southeast Asia to sample some of the best food this region has to offer? Would you come with me?

These questions were the inspiration for our television series, *Entrée To Asia*. After every visit I made to Southeast Asia friends would invariably ask me how my holiday was. For me, it was always a working holiday, traveling to learn and to eat. This style of voyage has had its ups and downs and, strangely, it has been mostly a solo adventure. Visiting markets and street stalls looking for culinary inspiration was rarely top of the agenda of most tourists I have met while on the road. I guess some people just prefer the beach.

So it was that, as I journeyed alone, I would fantasize about a television show that would share the streets and small out-of-the-way restaurants I have visited over the years with people like myself. People like you who now hold this book. I didn't really expect that it would be me hosting the show of my dreams, but life is full of surprises.

What is Entrée To Asia?

Think of it as a favorite recipe, a recipe that just happens to contain a little history, some culture, great cooking and travel — lots of travel. I take you out of your kitchen and put you right in the middle of the action: from Bangkok and Singapore, to Hong Kong, Kuala Lumpur and points east. *Entrée To Asia* is an entertaining television series about the food of Southeast Asia. This cookbook will give you recipes from the show that you're going to want to share with your friends, along with some of the stories about the people and places we encountered while we were there.

I said that I'd take you out of your kitchen. Well, *Entrée To Asia* will also send you back in to your kitchen — confident and equipped with the tools and techniques necessary to make your next food adventure so successful your friends and family will wonder where you've been. Unless of course they've seen the TV program. In which case, your secret's out of the bag!

— *Thomas Robson*

DEDICATION

Much can be communicated in a dedication: praise, thanks, acknowledgment and respect come to mind. I would like to give the reader an idea of the role these people had in the creation of this book. Quite simply, without them it could never have happened. Not any of it.

So please share my gratitude for the guidance, inspiration and assistance through many years from these eight individuals:

Sandra Robson, Jerry Libin, Carol Franchi, Fontaine Wong, John Cathro, Melanie Reffes, Leo Foucault, Randolph Eustace-Walden

What draws those of us who love to cook to the cuisines of Asia? The top two reasons on my list are adventure and magic. The adventure of exploring Chinatown and the other Asian neighborhoods in my hometown of Vancouver was certainly what drew me to experiment with Cantonese cuisine when I was a young boy, responsible for the evening meal for our small family. Those early trials were rewarding for me, but not necessarily for those who had to eat that experimental cuisine. Regardless, I was hooked on an exotic adventure, and it wasn't long before I realized I needed solid information. And so, after reading a neglected copy of a Chinese cookbook that had sat on our bookshelf for years, I discovered the magic of cooking something delicious.

Whether you are preparing meals three times a day for family, or entertaining from your kitchen occasionally, you still need adventure and magic to make it worthwhile for yourself as the cook and for the people you are feeding.

Adventure is fraught with peril you say? So be it. However, forewarned is forearmed. This collection of recipes will certainly mitigate that peril you will face in the kitchen. You must be willing to make mistakes in the kitchen. One of my first instructors at l'Institut de Tourisme et d'Hôtellerie du Québec told me that without mistakes, nothing genuinely new is learned! In fact you shouldn't worry; many have already trod the path you are about to take. It is now easier than ever to find the right ingredients to be able to enjoy this adventure and taste the magic for yourself.

The idea of East meets West cuisine has created quite a furor in culinary circles over the years. During the taping of *Entrée To Asia* we attended the World Gourmet Summit on the subject of "New Asian Cuisine." Chefs from all over the world flew into Singapore to participate in this panel discussion. There was very little agreement among the bright lights of the culinary world on this subject. But they were rooted in the present, and it seems to me they had a lack of perspective. Fusion cuisine (that is, the blending of different ethnic cuisines) is not the property of five-star chefs with big names. History tells us that the best examples (those that actually taste great) come from families in which two or more cultures have come together through marriage.

When we in the West look at Southeast Asia, we tend to see a group of countries and their similarities. We see a whole that Southeast Asians themselves would never imagine. The people who live there know better. Southeast Asia is an ancient part of the world, and different ethnic and cultural groups have been coming together there for a very long time. When they came together they did it over the cooking fires of the kitchen.

Many of the regional cuisines of this part of the world are, in fact, fusion cuisines. In Malaysia, for example, much of the most popular street food is Peranakan cuisine: a fusion cuisine born of indigenous Malay plus Chinese and Southern Indian influences. The food served in Thailand has been greatly influenced over the centuries by ingredients and cooking styles adapted from those of Sri Lanka, Burma, China and Portugal. There are many other examples throughout the region.

When you shop at your local Vietnamese, Lao or Chinese market and begin to share and explore Southeast Asian cooking customs, you are taking part in the same fusion dynamic. Perhaps one day, your family, too, will be a fusion family, and a new cuisine will be born of which your descendants can be justifiably proud.

Most Southeast Asian meals emphasize variety over quantity, enjoying several small tastes as part of a larger meal. The recipes in this book are scaled to serve four people as part of a menu of two or three dishes, some fresh fruit and rice. Soup is always welcome at an Asian meal, and it is usually served along with the other courses. Most noodle dishes are usually served on their own as a light lunch or a snack.

Set the table using your favorite plates. I like using soup or pasta plates as they are deep enough to hold a good amount of rice and keep the sauce from the curry where it belongs. Throughout Singapore, Malaysia and Thailand you rarely see chopsticks at the dinner table. Most meals are eaten with a spoon in the right hand and a fork in the left. The fork is used to help scoop food onto the spoon, and the spoon is used in the usual manner. Chopsticks are used only when eating at a Chinese restaurant, or at a noodle stand, where the mechanical advantage they provide over slippery noodles is greatly appreciated.

Don't worry a great deal about serving food piping hot. Meals are generally served all at once, and people serve themselves from the different platters, as they choose. You can prepare much of the food ahead of time, and then perhaps prepare a stir-fried dish at the last moment to bring out with the rest of the meal. Soups, however, should be served nice and hot.

The ideal beverage to accompany Southeast Asian fare is a glass of either water or fresh juice. Southeast Asians will also often enjoy a cold lager beer with the spiciest food. I prefer a nice pint of ale with most of the food in this book. The sweeter, caramel flavors of traditional English and American ales go a long way to balance the heat of Asian cuisines. In Thailand, many people prefer a weak but refreshing drink of whiskey and soda over lots of ice. Use a scant ½ oz/50 mL of whiskey with a full tumbler of soda and ice.

Do not make your kitchen time unpleasant. Try serving a dish from this book along with a simple grilled, roasted or pan-fried dish you are already familiar with. Incorporate these dishes into your regular menus to become familiar with them. With time you will probably find yourself incorporating elements of these recipes into dishes of your own creation. This is undoubtedly the best way to cook, as you are creating something that is truly your own. Do not be afraid to make mistakes — you cannot learn anything truly new if you do not push the limits.

In the West there still exists a mystique that all Asian chefs meticulously prepare all their ingredients in the ancestral manner. While this remains so for those with the patience to do so, many Asian home chefs, like you and I, are hard pressed to find the time. They opt for the convenience offered by packets of prepared spices, such as those made by Asian Home Gourmet. When you see this symbol **é** in a recipe, look to the back of the book for the name of the Asian Home Gourmet SpicePaste™ that can be substituted for the handmade spice paste or spice mix.

CHAPTER I

ingaporean food: a misleading statement. While there are a few dishes that are considered typically Singaporean, there really isn't a single Singaporean cuisine. There are, however, a lot of Singaporean gourmets. Not your typical blue-blooded nose in the air, money to spare kind of gourmet. I'm talking about everyday people doing everyday jobs who will stop what they are doing to discuss the minute details of what makes a certain dish "right". During a visit I made to a Singaporean tailor a culinary discussion broke out that nearly shut the store. Forget the fitting I was there for; I was kicking myself for not having a tape recorder handy to catch the pearls of kitchen wisdom that were traded back and forth by these everyday gourmets. I'll know better next time.

Singapore is the ideal place to begin your Southeast Asian eating adventure. The variety Singapore has to offer is stunning. You can snack for pennies at hawker centers or spend hundreds on a meal for one. And all of it is of a quality that constantly surprises.

Singapore is both a city and a country – a city state – comprising a small island at the tip of the Malay Peninsula. It is a small country built on commerce, and through dedication and efficiency has become one of the most affluent countries in Asia.

The cleanliness and sense of order of Singapore comes as a shock when you compare this country to other parts of Asia. For this reason alone it can be seen as a nice break from the more hectic pace you find elsewhere in this part of the world. Although Singapore's culture and roots date back centuries, make no mistake, it is a very modern country in its present incarnation, barely 35 years old. You may find yourself searching back alleys and old parts of town to get acquainted with that original old-world culture, but isn't that what great travel experiences are made of?

Some aspects of Singapore have hardly changed at all, and fortunately for us this includes traditional "wet markets." The name comes from the practice of using ice to keep the fresh produce, meat and seafood in top condition. The result is wet and sometimes slippery floors; a throwback to earlier days before there were supermarkets. Food-serious Singaporeans would have it no other way.

Orchard Road at dusk

A Singapore wet market is a chef's dream come true. All manner of vegetables, poultry, meat and spices are on sale here. The best of everything, freshest and most fragrant, brought together for you to pick and choose. Even the simplest menu plans begin to grow to banquet proportions as you are tempted by the excellent selection. A visit to a wet market would definitely qualify as a great travel experience. The buying and selling is frantic; your senses will be positively reeling. And the seafood!

If you go to one of Singapore's wet markets, and you simply must, go hungry. Most have a hawkers' area where you can buy local cuisine, ready to eat. So, after a morning or an afternoon of exploring, surrounded by food, you can quench your thirst and fill your belly!

Once upon a time in Singapore, not so long ago, at the end of the business day people would hurry to move their automobiles out of parking-lots and off certain back streets in order to make room for the arrival of the Hawker Carts. As the sun began to set, it was time for the "night market" to open! The *pasar malam*, or night market, was an exciting place for people to go. Soon they would be meeting with family and old friends. Laughing, shopping and, inevitably, eating until it was time to go home, often well after midnight. Now that Singapore is a modern city the old streetside eating and shopping has largely been done away with. Mercifully, it has been replaced by local "hawker's centers."

A hawkers' center is a covered but otherwise open air setting where hawkers (street vendors) compete for your attention, each of them serving up local snacks and specialties. The competition for tastebuds is vocal and more than a little frenetic. You never know where a hawkers' center might be found. Just follow your nose and you might find 20 or 30 hawkers set up permanently (as opposed to the old fashioned mobile manner), tucked away in a park, or downstairs in a popular mall, or on the open air second floor of a housing block.

If you travel to Singapore there is one aspect of their culture that you simply must seek out, and that is Peranakan cuisine. What is Peranakan? Simply put, Chinese merchants intermarried with local Malay and Southern Indian families in order to be better involved in the lucrative spice trade and other commerce of the region. One of the results of this intermarriage was the cuisine of these new Peranakan families. In fact, it's an excellent example of a genuine fusion cuisine created more than a century ago by families rather than restaurants.

A Nonya is a woman of the Peranakan culture. What makes their cuisine so remarkable is the pride that Malays, Chinese and Indians all have for their own cookery, and how that pride became amplified in the kitchens of the Nonya matriarchs. Every Nonya had unique family recipes, those she created herself and those created by her mother, her aunts and her grandmother. In the old days the family cuisine had a big impact on the status of the family in the community.

Hours of careful work go into the preparation of this aristocratic family cuisine. Over the years many secrets and techniques of Peranakan cookery have been lost. People no longer have the time or the big extended family homes that make this complex cuisine possible. In an ironic twist, this very family-oriented cuisine is now better suited to restaurant production methods, and many popular hawker dishes have their origins in the Peranakan kitchen. So if you find a Peranakan restaurant or if you are invited to eat in a Singapore Nonya's home, consider it a privilege and a treat.

Every year, for the entire month of July, chefs, food educators and restaurateurs from all over the world descend on Singapore for the International Food Festival. They come here to learn about new food trends, compete for culinary awards and share insights and information. But mostly, they come to eat, here, where the concept of Asian food is developed to a fine art.

CURRY NOODLES

There are popular curry noodle dishes from Singapore, Penang and Chiang Mai. Wherever you go, the idea is the same: a fusion of Chinese noodles and an Indian-inspired gravy served in a bowl by a street-side vendor. In Singapore you might savor Assam Laksa, a spicy fish broth flavored with tamarind, pineapple and fresh mint. Singapore Laksa is also made with fish and is flavored with coconut milk and banana blossom. Khao Soi is the popular version from Chiang Mai, Thailand, and can be made with chicken or pork. This curry noodle dish is influenced by all three versions. A delicious one-dish meal.

SPICE PASTE

3 in/7.5 cm of lemon grass, minced
2 large red chilies, minced,
    or 2 tsp/10 mL ground chili paste
2 candle nuts
½ in/1 cm cube of fresh galanga, minced
½ in/1 cm cube of fresh ginger
    root, minced
3 cloves garlic, minced
4 shallot onions, minced
¼ tsp/1 mL turmeric
2 tsp/10 mL shrimp paste

MAIN INGREDIENTS

3 tbsp/45 mL vegetable oil
½ lb/250 g boneless chicken, cut in cubes
3 cups/750 mL chicken stock
2 cups/500 mL thick coconut milk
Salt to taste
1 lb/500 g fresh egg noodles
8 cups/2 L boiling water

GARNISH

Fresh bean sprouts, trimmed and cleaned
    lime wedges, crisply fried shallot onions
    and dried chili flakes

COCONUT MILK

When you open a can of coconut milk, you will see that the rich cream has risen to the top. You can scoop the cream off the thinner milk below to be used separately in many recipes. If your recipe calls for thick coconut milk, just shake the can to mix the cream and milk together. Any unused cream or coconut milk can be refrigerated or frozen for later use.

METHOD

1. Prepare all ingredients and have at hand. Using a mortar and pestle or a small food processor or blender, pound or grind the spice paste ingredients in the order given until they form a coarse paste.

2. Preheat a large, heavy bottomed pan over medium heat. Add the oil, and when the oil is hot, add the spice paste and fry it until it becomes fragrant and no longer smells raw.

3. Add the chicken and fry for 3 to 5 minutes. Add the stock and bring to a boil. Reduce the heat and simmer for 20 minutes.

4. Add the coconut milk and salt and continue to simmer for another 5 minutes.

5. Meanwhile, in a large pan cook the egg noodles in the boiling water until just done (3 to 4 minutes from the time the water returns to a boil). Drain and very quickly rinse the noodles with running water. Drain well again and divide among the serving bowls.

6. Serve the curry over the freshly cooked noodles and garnish.

SENTOSA GRILLED BEEF AND GREENS

Sentosa Island is a resort just off the coast of Singapore. There are several large hotels and numerous activities to keep tourists and native Singaporeans occupied. But even in the midst of the tropical pitch-and-putt, the aroma of the grill assails you. This beef recipe suits a number of leafy greens. Try it with mustard or beet greens, kale, gai lan or rappini. The work of chef Tracy Cooper of Vancouver, Canada, inspired this dish.

SEASONING

4 cloves garlic, mashed
1 tsp/5 mL turmeric
2 tsp/10 mL coriander powder
1 tsp/5 mL cumin powder
1 tbsp/15 mL chili flakes, or chili powder
4 tsp/20 mL sugar
2 tsp/10 mL salt
1 tbsp/15 mL fish sauce
2 tsp/10 mL sweet soy sauce
4 tsp/20 mL oil

MAIN INGREDIENTS

1 flank steak, 1 lb/400 - 500 g
Boiling water
1 ½ lb/700 g fresh, leafy greens washed
    and trimmed, stalks cut in bite sized
    pieces, leaves separated from stalks
Suitable leafy greens could include
    mustard greens, kale, gai lan, rapini,
    beet greens, alone or in combination.
2 tbsp/30 mL oil
3 cloves garlic, crushed
2 tsp/10 mL Chinese wine, or whiskey
Sesame oil, few drops

METHOD

1. In a mortar and pestle pound the four cloves of garlic and combine the remaining seasoning ingredients. Marinate the flank steak in this mixture for least one hour. You can preheat a grill or barbecue while the flank steak marinates.

2. Briefly blanch the stalks in a large pan of boiling water, and then cool them under cold running water. Drain the stalks well. Have all remaining ingredients prepared and at hand.

3. Grill the flank steak over medium high heat until rare or medium rare. Alternatively, you can fry the steak in a heavy frying pan. Allow to rest on a plate while you finish the recipe.

4. Preheat a wok or large heavy frying pan until hot and add the 2 tbsp/25 mL oil. When the oil is hot add the 3 crushed cloves of garlic and a moment later the blanched stalks. Stir-fry for a few moments and then add the leaves. Sprinkle the Chinese wine over the greens along with the sesame oil. Any juices accumulated in the dish from the steak should be added as well. Mix well and turn off the heat.

5. Arrange the stir-fried greens in a serving dish and keep warm. Slice the flank steak into narrow strips against the grain. Lay the flank steak strips on top of the greens and serve.

RED CURRY PASTE CHICKEN BREAST
WITH GLASS NOODLE SALAD

 lass noodles, or bean threads, are a real wonder food of Asia. They are made from the protein of mung beans and contain no starch or gluten, so they are ideal for special diets. For dishes with lengthy cooking times, the noodles won't fall apart the way flour-based noodles will. The real advantage to glass noodles is that they require no cooking. Just soak them for 15 minutes and then drain them well.

SEASONING

1 to 2 tbsp/15 to 30 mL Thai red
    curry paste
1 tbsp/15 mL fish sauce
2 tbsp/30 mL fresh lime juice
2 tsp/10 mL sugar
Salt, pinch
1 to 2 red chilies, sliced thinly

MAIN INGREDIENTS

2 small bundles of mung bean noodles
    (about 3 oz/85 g)
⅓ cup/75 mL cucumber, cut into
    matchstick-size pieces
⅓ cup/75 mL fresh bean sprouts, trimmed
2 tbsp/30 mL fresh mint, coarsely chopped
2 tbsp/30 mL green onion, sliced thinly
2 chicken breasts, about ¼ to
    ½ lb/125 to 250 g each

GARNISH
Sprigs of fresh mint and wedges of lime

METHOD

1. Marinate the chicken breasts in the Thai curry paste for least 1 hour. Soak the mung bean noodles in hot water for 15 to 20 minutes. Drain. Prepare all remaining ingredients and have at hand.

2. Mix the mung bean noodles, cucumber, bean sprouts, mint and green onions in a bowl.

3. Combine the remaining seasoning ingredients and stir until the sugar and salt are dissolved. Add this mixture to the noodles and vegetables. (At this stage, the salad can be chilled for up to 2 hours or used right away.)

4. Preheat a nonstick frying pan over medium-high heat and fry the chicken breasts until done. Set aside on a plate.

5. While the chicken breasts cool, arrange the salad on a platter or, if you prefer, divide it among several plates.

6. Slice the chicken breasts into 5 or 6 pieces crosswise and arrange them on top of the salad. Garnish and serve.

SEARED SALMON
WITH THAI FRAGRANT RICE

y good friend chef Karl Eibensteiner provided the inspiration for this fusion presentation. Enjoy this low-fat entrée with a side salad for a very flavorful and healthful lunch or supper.

SEASONING

2 tsp/10 mL dried chili flakes
2 tbsp/30 mL fresh lime juice
4 tsp/20 mL fish sauce
4 to 5 tsp/20 to 25 mL sugar
1 to 2 tsp/5 to 10 mL lemon grass,
   finely minced

MAIN INGREDIENTS

3 cups/750 mL freshly cooked rice
¼ cup/50 mL coconut milk powder
   (see sidebar)
¼ cup/50 mL combined: finely diced
   sweet red and yellow peppers and
   thinly sliced green onion
12 slices of salmon, ½ inch/1 cm
   thick each

METHOD

1. In a non-reactive bowl combine the seasoning ingredients and stir well until the sugar dissolves.

2. Preheat a non-stick frying pan over high heat and when hot fry the salmon pieces until bronze colored, turning them over once only. Meanwhile, prepare the rice.

3. Combine the freshly cooked rice with the coconut powder and diced vegetables. Lightly dress the rice with a few teaspoons of the seasoning per person. Press about ¾ cup/175 mL of hot rice into a small cup or bowl for each person and then unmold onto a warm plate.

4. Arrange the cooked salmon beside the rice and serve.

POWDER OR MILK?

Coconut milk powder has all the flavor of quality coconut milk, but with a lower fat content. Modern spray dehydrating methods limit the amount of fat that is present in the powder form — a great alternative for rich, full-fat coconut milk.

SRI LANKAN LOBSTER CURRY

The popularity of Sri Lankan Buddhism had a profound effect on neighboring cultures. Their cuisine as well as their philosophy traveled far and wide. Should you ever visit Singapore, be sure to sample the wonderful Southern Indian food available there. The kari leaves are an important ingredient, but if you cannot find them, just leave them out. The lobster is a nice substitute for the huge prawns available in Southeast Asia, but feel free to substitute other seafood or fish if you wish.

SPICE PASTE

½ tsp/2 mL fenugreek seed
¼ tsp/1 mL fennel seed
2 medium green chilies, chopped
2 cloves garlic, chopped
1 slice ginger (about the thickness of
     a quarter), chopped
2 tsp/10 mL coriander powder
1 tbsp/15 mL chili powder
½ tsp/2 mL tamarind pulp

SEASONING

1 inch/2.5 cm of cinnamon stick
5 to 10 fresh kari leaves
4 large shallot onions, sliced
1 tsp/5 mL salt

MAIN INGREDIENTS

2 to 3 lbs/1 to 1.5 kg fresh lobster, killed and
     segmented with claws and joints cracked
2 - 14 oz/400 mL cans of coconut milk,
     separated (Both the thick cream and the
     thinner milk will be used.)

GARNISH

Sprigs of fresh coriander

METHOD

1. Using a mortar and pestle or a small blender or food processor, pound or grind the spice paste ingredients in the order given until they form a coarse paste. Prepare all remaining ingredients and have at hand.

2. Preheat a wok or other deep, heavy bottomed pan over medium-high heat, then add about ½ cup/125 mL thick coconut cream. Reduce the cream while stirring until it has thoroughly separated and there is almost no steam coming from the pan.

3. Add the spice paste, cinnamon stick, kari leaves, sliced shallot onions and salt and stir. Continue to cook for a moment while the spice paste imparts its flavor to the coconut fat.

4. Add the lobster pieces and stir gently, cooking over medium-high heat for 3 to 4 minutes. Add the thinner coconut milk and bring to a boil. Simmer the lobster for 5 to 10 minutes or until done. Enrich the sauce by adding enough thick coconut cream to give a rich, creamy texture. (Any remaining thick coconut cream can be frozen for future use.)

5. Taste the sauce and adjust the seasoning adding a pinch of sugar or salt as desired. Serve immediately garnished with the fresh coriander.

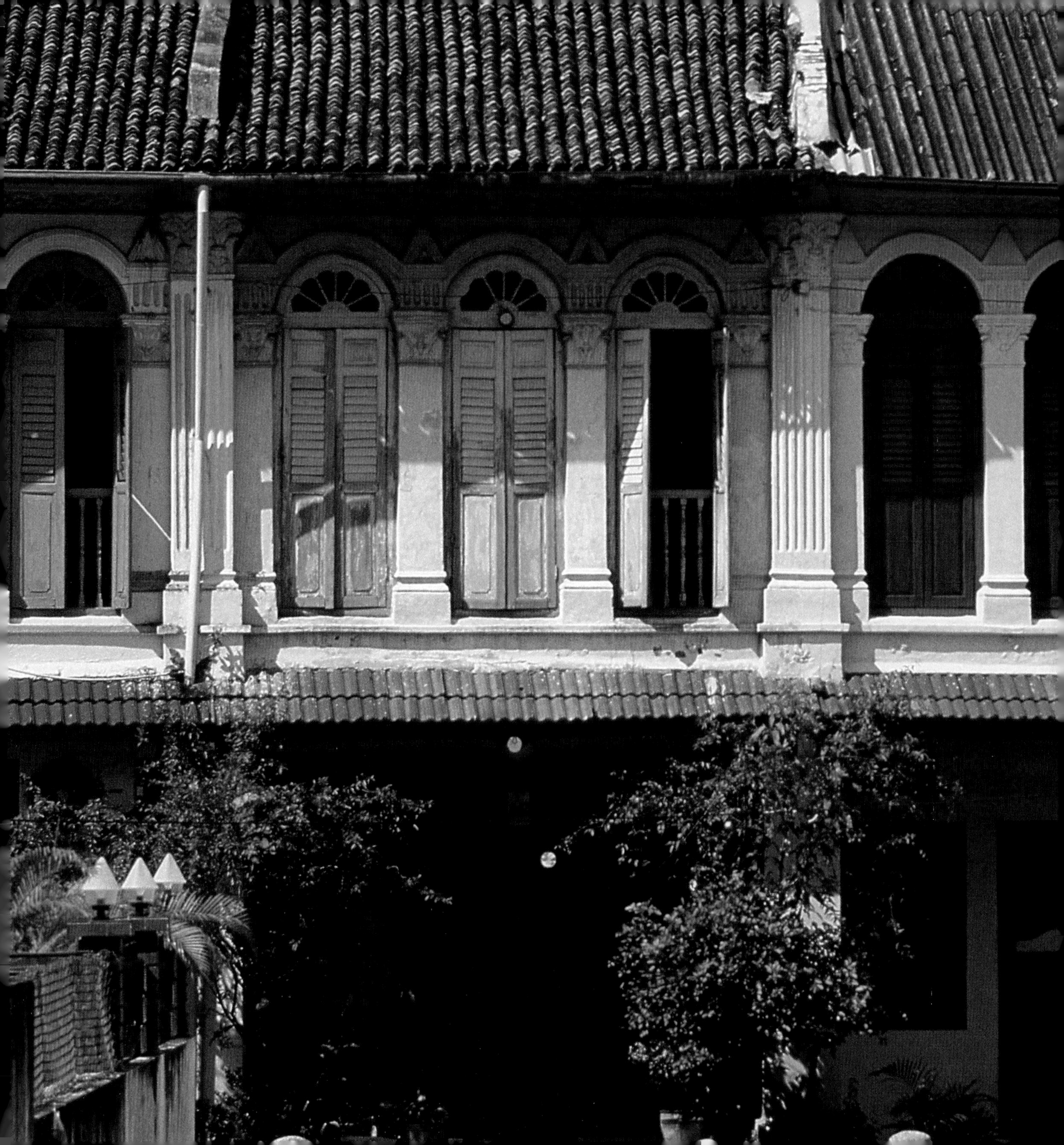

SAMBAL MUSSELS

his is a typical Malay sambal. The sauce is based on a home-style rempah (Malay for fresh spice paste). If you want to add your own touch, try substituting other spice pastes from this cookbook (or even store-bought ones).

SPICE PASTE

4 candle nuts or macadamia nuts
3 large fresh red chilies, finely minced
 or 1 tbsp/15 ml ground chili paste
2 cloves garlic, finely chopped
4 shallot onions, finely minced
2 tsp/10 mL shrimp paste

SEASONING

1 tbsp/15 mL fish sauce
¼ cup/60 mL tamarind water
½ cup/125 mL coconut milk
1 to 2 tbsp/15 to 30 mL sugar, or to taste

MAIN INGREDIENTS

2 to 3 tbsp/30 to 45 mL vegetable oil
1 lb/500 g fresh mussels, trimmed and cleaned
2 sprigs of fresh basil, Thai or other,
 coarsely chopped
GARNISH
Sprigs of fresh basil and sliced red chilies

METHOD

1. Using a mortar and pestle or a small blender or food processor, pound or grind the spice paste ingredients in the order given until they form a coarse paste. Prepare all remaining ingredients and have at hand.

2. Preheat a wok or other deep, heavy-bottomed pan over high heat. Add the oil. As soon is the oil is hot, add the spice paste and stir well to combine. Continue to cook for 1 minute while the spice paste imparts its flavor to the oil.

3. Add the fish sauce, tamarind water, coconut milk and sugar. Stir until the mixture comes to boil.

4. Add the mussels. Continue to stir, coating the mussels with the sauce until it returns to a boil. Cover the pan and cook until the mussels open, about 4 minutes.

5. Discard any mussels that do not open. Add the basil and stir. Taste the sauce and adjust the seasoning. Add more sugar or fish sauce as desired.

6. Garnish and serve immediately.

PERANAKAN PANCAKES

The Peranakan culture appears Chinese at first, but there is an unmistakable Southern Indian influence – especially in the cuisine. In Southern India, these small pancakes would be called *Apom* and might be served alongside a breakfast curry or other savory dish. This Peranakan version pairs the pancakes with a memorable sauce of rich coconut milk, palm sugar and bananas. For a change of pace, prepare them without the sauce and serve them with your favorite fiery curry.

MAIN INGREDIENTS

For the banana sauce:
1 cup/250 mL thick coconut milk
3 oz/100 mL water
5 oz/150 g palm sugar
Salt, pinch
2 pandan leaves (optional)
2 to 3 ripe bananas
1 tbsp/15 ml cornstarch,
    dissolved in 2 tbsp/30 ml water

For the pancake:
2 ¾ cups/300 g rice flour
½ tsp/2.5 ml salt
1 tbsp/15 ml sugar
1 tsp/5 ml instant yeast
2 ½ cups/570 mL thick
    coconut milk

METHOD

1. Sift together the rice flour, salt, sugar and yeast. Stir in the thick coconut milk to create a smooth batter. Leave the batter to rise in a warm corner for 45 minutes to 1 hour, or until the batter is quite foamy.

2. Meanwhile, prepare the banana sauce. In a small non-reactive pan combine the coconut milk, water, palm sugar, salt, pandan leaves and bananas and bring the mixture to a boil. Lower the heat and simmer the sauce until the palm sugar is dissolved. Remove the pandan leaves and discard them. Thicken the sauce with enough of the cornstarch solution to give a creamy texture that coats the back of a spoon. Keep the sauce warm.

3. Preheat a very small non-stick skillet over medium-high heat and grease it lightly. Ladle in ¼ cup of the batter and tilt the pan to coat the bottom evenly. Cook the pancake on one side only, keeping the pan covered until the pancake is cooked through.

4. Repeat step 3 until the pancake batter is used up. Serve the pancakes with the banana sauce ladled over top.

CHAPTER 2

Malaysia

Malaysia manages to convey a low-key, relaxed ambiance that made our time there pleasurable indeed. In contrast to urbanized Singaporean chefs, many of Malaysia's specialists were shy by comparison. Once you get a chance to sample typical Malaysian food, however, you will come to believe that their modesty is misplaced. Malaysia's streets and kitchens are perfumed by steaming pots of delicious food and ambrosial coffee and tea. Tea is taken so seriously there that there are regular competitions for those who make the famous "pulled tea." Pulled tea is a milky, sweet concoction that is skillfully poured or "pulled" from one beaker to another until it develops a rich frothy head. Competition amongst tea pullers is fierce, and it is not unusual to see a skilled tea-master pulling tea from two or more stainless steel jugs at the same time. To see these talented individuals defy the laws of fluid dynamics is amazing.

My ideal Kuala Lumpur breakfast would feature pulled tea and freshly made *roti canai*. Roti canai (pronounced rotee chanai) is a wonderful flat-bread made to order right before your eyes. A small blob of dough is stretched and then flipped repeatedly until it is as thin as strudel pastry. The now huge sheet of paper-thin dough is carefully twisted into a flat cake that is pan-fried until golden brown. The resulting flat-bread is multi-layered and flaky with contrasting crisp and seductively silky textures. Roti canai is served with a very mild curry so that you can dip the still-hot pieces of bread into the sauce to soak up the goodness. Perfect accompaniment to a big hot mug of tea!

Malaysia offers the hungry traveler a wonderful opportunity to eat on the street. In Kuala Lumpur, the night market in Chinatown and the famous street Jalan Alor are two ideal places to dine alfresco.

If you ever get the chance to visit Malaysia, the historic city of Georgetown, on the island of Penang, is not to be missed. Georgetown is a haven for the hybrid Peranakan (also often referred to as Nonya) cuisine. Most people travel to Penang for the tourist hotels and resorts which are located on the far side of the island. But by avoiding Georgetown they miss the oldest British colonial outpost on the Malay peninsula and a city rich in historical significance. Today, it's just as likely to

The Temple of the Iron Goddess of Mercy, Penang, Malaysia

be visited by high-tech professionals, for Penang is quickly becoming a Southeast Asian version of Silicon Valley. It's a good bet that if you own a personal computer, some part of it was made there.

Melaka, the ancient port city, with its Portuguese and Dutch influences, is also a popular destination appreciated for the diverse architecture, culture and cuisine that can be sampled there. Melaka's Portuguese community is well over 400 years old. In the older parts of town, elegant Sino-Portuguese homes and shop-houses have been turned into guest houses offering a low-cost opportunity to experience a lifestyle that is fast being replaced by Western-style progress. The food served in the Malay/Portuguese restaurants in Melaka is especially delicious.

India, too – Southern India especially – has had a remarkable influence on the cultures of Southeast Asia. After a busy morning shooting in Melaka we decided to have a quick lunch in a typical Southern Indian cafeteria. A row of washbasins lined one wall so we could wash our hands. All seven of us sat at a long table topped with polished stainless steel. Within moments of sitting down, large pieces of clean banana leaf were placed in front of us and a portion of rice and several varieties of vegetable were served right on the leaf. Then the waiter came by to offer us a selection of meat, fish or chicken dishes to complete the meal. Forks and spoons were politely offered and, I'm proud to say, politely refused. By this point in our journey our crew worked and ate together, even if it meant eating with our bare hands. We had all become pilgrims on this culinary *satori*.

Before heading off to Malaysia it was suggested to me by some friends that Kuala Lumpur, the capital city, was nothing more than a modern-day metropolis shadowed by towers of glass, concrete and steel. The soaring, multi-storied Petronus Towers are a particularly awesome sight, especially at night. Fortunately, even in this modern city center, you can find excellent food served to both rich and poor alike at small tables and stalls set up by food hawkers in the street and in the increasingly popular food centers. These serious traditionalists are not about to let their culinary history disappear, even in the heart of metropolitan Kuala Lumpur.

When you dine at a hawker stall you are eating with a specialist. Hawkers generally offer only one dish or kind of food in an effort to excel at that item and thereby squeeze out local competition. The streetside lifestyle that hawkers live is as much a challenge as running a small restaurant. Fortunately, in KL many people prefer good hawker fare to franchise chicken and burgers.

Pristine beaches, lush mountain forests and national parks make Malaysia a must-see destination. But as far as I'm concerned, it's in its kitchens where this country really shines.

STIR-FRIED FRESH BROAD RICE NOODLES

Fresh broad rice noodles are pre-cooked, glossy white and about ¾ of an inch wide. They are a favorite stir-fry staple of street vendors since they only need to be seasoned and thoroughly heated through. You will find them refrigerated in many Asian markets and supermarkets. When they are very fresh the noodles are soft and pliable. When refrigerated they become quite firm, but once heated, they are tender and flexible again. You can try this recipe with red onions, carrots and cabbage if peppers aren't available.

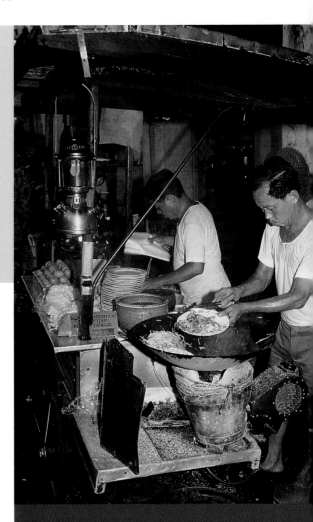

SEASONING

2 cloves garlic, minced
2 fresh red chilies, minced
2 tsp/10 mL Chinese wine, or whiskey
4 to 6 tsp/20 to 30 mL fish sauce
1 to 2 tbsp/15 to 30 mL sweet soy sauce

MAIN INGREDIENTS

3 to 4 tbsp/45 to 60 mL vegetable oil
1 ½ to 2 cups/375 to 500 mL julienne
   of sweet peppers, assorted colors
1 lb/500 g fresh broad rice noodles,
   loosened
1 cup/250 mL fresh bean sprouts, trimmed

GARNISH

Coarsely chopped green onion and fresh
   coriander tossed with finely sliced red
   chili. (You'll need at least ½ cup/
   125 mL of this mixture.)

METHOD

1. Prepare all ingredients and have at hand.

2. Preheat a wok or a large, heavy frying pan over high heat. Add oil.

3. As soon as the oil is hot, add the garlic and chilies. Stir once or twice, then add the peppers. Continue to stir-fry for a few minutes while sprinkling the Chinese wine and some fish sauce over the mixture.

4. Add the rice noodles and continue to cook, mixing the noodles with the peppers while sprinkling more fish sauce over everything.

5. When the noodles are heated through, drizzle the soy sauce over top and add the bean sprouts. Toss the noodles and mix well. Transfer to a serving plate, garnish and serve.

SOUTHERN INDIAN CHICK PEA CURRY

T his is real southern Indian comfort food, bringing together all kinds of aromatic ingredients in a rich, creamy sauce that is wonderful with freshly cooked rice. It is not complicated and is a great introduction to many important ingredients in Southeast Asian cookery and to how they are used. This recipe can be made ahead and refrigerated: the flavor will improve over 48 hours. It freezes well, too.

SEASONING

½ inch/1.25 cm piece of cinnamon stick
1 piece star anise
5 to 6 fresh kari leaves
2 inch/5 cm piece lemon grass
4 shallot onions, sliced
2 large red chilies, sliced
   or 1 tsp/5mL chili flakes
1 tbsp/15 mL coriander powder
2 tsp/10 mL cumin powder
½ tsp/2 mL turmeric
3 to 4 tbsp/45 to 60 mL tamarind water

MAIN INGREDIENTS

2 tbsp/30 mL oil
1 large can chick peas, rinsed and drained
1 ½ to 2 cups/375 to 500 mL coconut milk
1 to 2 tbsp/15 to 30 mL dark palm sugar
   or 1 tbsp/15 mL brown sugar
Salt to taste
2 to 3 tbsp/30 to 45 mL fresh coriander,
   chopped

GARNISH
Fresh coriander leaves

METHOD

1. Prepare all ingredients and have at hand. Preheat heavy-bottomed pan over medium-high heat. Add oil.

2. When the oil is hot, add the cinnamon, star anise, kari leaves and lemon grass. Stir for about 10 seconds. Allow these ingredients to sizzle while they impart their flavor to the oil. Do not allow any burning.

3. Add the shallot onions and chilies and continue to stir until the onions become fragrant.

4. Add the coriander powder, cumin powder and tumeric and stir for another 5 to 10 seconds. Do not burn.

5. Add the chick peas, tamarind water, 1 ½ cups/375 mL coconut milk and sugar and bring the curry to a boil (Add more coconut milk or water if you prefer a thinner curry.) Reduce heat and simmer uncovered for 15 to 20 minutes.

6. Taste and adjust the seasoning adding more sugar, salt or even a squeeze of fresh lime juice as desired. Add the chopped coriander, stir and garnish.

COCONUT RICE

I've had coconut rice from Mexico, Jamaica and Trinidad, but Malaysian coconut rice takes the prize. This makes a great side dish on all sorts of menus, not just Asian ones. Try it with grilled or roast chicken.

SEASONING

3 pandan leaves
½ inch/1 cm cube of fresh
   ginger root, finely chopped
2 small shallot onions, finely chopped
1 small clove garlic, finely chopped
1 small stick cinnamon
2 cloves
2 tsp/10 mL salt

MAIN INGREDIENTS

2 ½ cups/625 mL long grain rice,
   washed and drained
2 cups/500 mL coconut milk.
3 cups/750 mL water.

METHOD

1. Prepare all ingredients and have at hand. Clean the pandan leaves and tie each one in a knot.

2. In a heavy pan, combine all ingredients and seasonings. Bring the mixture to a boil uncovered, stirring occasionally. Continue to cook the mixture, boiling for 3 to 4 minutes. Be sure to stir to prevent scorching.

3. Reduce the heat to low and cover the pan. Continue to cook the rice for 15 to 20 minutes without uncovering the pan.

4. Open the pan and gently fluff the rice with a fork. Remove the pandan leaves, cinnamon stick and cloves. Cover the pan again and let the rice sit for 10 to 15 minutes before serving.

FRESH FISH GRILLED IN A BANANA LEAF

t was the beautiful aroma of this dish that drew me to the hawker stall in Kuala Lumpur where it was being prepared. The fellow who made it for us pointed out that it takes a careful hand with the heat to insure the fish cooks without scorching the banana leaf; try using a big cast-iron frying pan. Any type of flat fish or fish steak suits this recipe, and feel free to try other spice pastes and seasonings.

SPICE PASTE

1 stalk lemon grass, finely minced
3 slices galanga, finely minced
3 large fresh red chilies, finely minced,
   or 1 tbsp/15 mL ground chili paste
4 cloves garlic, finely minced
2 large shallot onions, finely minced
2 tbsp/30 mL shrimp paste

ě

MAIN INGREDIENTS

1 to 1 ½ pounds/500 to 750 g
   fresh fish cleaned, scaled and gutted
3 to 4 tbsp/45 to 60 mL vegetable oil
Banana leaves, fresh or frozen
GARNISH
Small peeled shallot onions, fresh chilies
   and lime wedges

METHOD

1. Prepare all ingredients and have at hand. Using a mortar and pestle or a small blender or food processor, pound or grind the spice paste ingredients in the order given until they form a coarse paste.

2. In a small pan heat 3 to 4 tbsp/45 to 50 mL oil until hot and add the spice paste. Cook, stirring until the aroma is fragrant; about 4 to 5 minutes. Cool.

3. Cut 2 or 3 sections of the banana leaf large enough to fold over the fish, then wipe them clean with a damp cloth. Spread half the fried spice paste over the banana leaf where you want to place the fish. Place the fish on top of paste and spread remaining paste on top of the fish. Fold the banana leaf over the fish.

4. Heat a large, heavy-bottomed frying pan over medium heat and add 1-2 tbsp/15-30 mL oil. Carefully place the fish into the pan and cook each side 10 to 15 minutes depending on the thickness of the fish. Turn the entire package of fish and banana leaf over. If the banana leaf begins to scorch or burn, lower the heat, and slip another piece of banana leaf underneath to protect the fish, and continue cooking.

5. Serve accompanied by the raw shallot onions, fresh chilies and lime.

SAMBAL FISH

ou can find this classic dish anywhere in Malaysia, Indonesia or Singapore. The sauce can be made ahead and refrigerated or frozen for later use. This dish is also great when the fish is grilled, steamed or pan fried with very little oil in a non-stick frying pan.

SPICE PASTE

10 peppercorns, fresh or dried
6 large red chilies, chopped/
   or 2 tbsp/30 mL ground chili paste
1 tbsp plus 2 tsp/25 mL chopped ginger
2 large cloves garlic, chopped
3 shallot onions, chopped

SEASONING

1 tbsp/15 mL fish sauce
3 tbsp/45 mL tamarind water
2 tbsp/30 mL palm or brown sugar
1 cup/250 mL coconut milk

MAIN INGREDIENTS

Medium-sized whole fresh fish,
   about 2 lbs/1 kg, cleaned and scaled
3 to 4 tbsp/45 to 60 mL fresh lime juice
2 tbsp/30 mL vegetable oil
Vegetable oil for shallow frying
GARNISH
Fresh Thai basil or sprigs of other fresh herbs
   and sliced red chilies

METHOD

1. Dry the fish with paper towel and sprinkle it inside and out with the lime juice. Set the fish aside, uncovered, while you prepare the rest of the ingredients.

2. Using a mortar and pestle or a small blender or food processor, pound or grind the spice paste ingredients in the order given until they form a coarse paste.

3. Preheat a wok or saucepan and add the 2 tbsp/25 mL of oil. When the oil is hot, fry the spice paste for 1 to 2 minutes or until fragrant.

4. Add the fish sauce, tamarind water and sugar and bring to boil. Add the coconut milk. Bring to a boil again. Lower the heat and simmer the sauce for 4 minutes. Taste and adjust seasoning, adding more fish sauce, sugar or lime as desired. Keep the sauce hot over low heat.

4. Heat the oil in a deep pan, suitable for shallow frying. Wipe any excess lime juice from the fish with some paper towel. When the oil is hot, shallow-fry the fish until golden on one side. Using tongs, carefully turn the fish over and cook the second side until golden and the fish is done. Carefully remove the fish from the pan and drain on paper towel before placing it on a platter.

5. Pour the sauce over the fish and garnish.

SAMBAL SQUID

etty Lim, culinary consultant to the Blue Ginger Peranakan Restaurant in Singapore, shared this recipe with us during the taping of *Entrée To Asia*. Letty is the most recent of a family line of famous Peranakan Nonya chefs. Traditionally, Peranakan cuisine was a time-consuming and elaborate affair, created by wealthy families to enhance status when entertaining, but this dish is easy to organize and quick to prepare.

SPICE PASTE

4 candle nuts or macedamia nuts
20 dried red chilies, soaked in 2 cups/
    500 mL boiling water to soften
    or 2 to 4 tbsp/30 to 60 mL ground
    chili paste
2 cloves garlic, finely chopped
5 shallot onions, finely minced
1 tbsp/15 mL shrimp paste

SEASONING

½ cup/125 mL tamarind water
2 tbsp/30 mL sugar
2 tsp/10 mL salt

INGREDIENTS

2 tbsp/30 mL vegetable oil
1 large onion, sliced
1 lb/500 g cleaned squid tubes,
    cut in ¼-inch/5-mm rings

METHOD

1. Using a mortar and pestle or a small blender or food processor, pound or grind the spice paste ingredients in the order given until they form a coarse paste. Prepare all remaining ingredients and have at hand.

2. Preheat a wok or other deep, heavy-bottomed pan over high heat. Add the oil. As soon as the oil is hot, add the spice paste and onion. Stir well to conbine. Continue to cook for 1 minute while the spice paste imparts its flavor to the oil.

3. Add the squid tubes and stir-fry over high heat for 1 minute or until the squid changes color. Add the tamarind water, sugar and salt.

4. Taste the sauce and adjust the seasoning, adding more sugar or salt as desired. Serve immediately.

CHAPTER 3

Entrée to Asia

Thailand

M y first love. Thai cuisine opened my senses to possibilities of flavor that I had only dreamed of. And the opportunity to learn! As a cook or chef Thailand constantly challenges and educates you. Everywhere you go, every street corner is dominated by hawker chefs who have dedicated their lives to mastering the preparation of the one or two dishes that will earn them a living.

Should you bring a notebook and a camera, Thailand's hawkers will teach you, by example, how to make dozens of dishes in a single day. What a way to travel: you can go anywhere in Thailand just nibbling and never sit down to a full-course meal. This country is a snacker's paradise! Nowhere have I seen such devotion on the part of chefs and such appreciation on the part of patrons than in the myriad eating establishments of this land.

Bangkok and the historic capitol Ayutthaya have both traditionally been called "The Venice of the East" because of their many canals and waterways. Centuries ago, Ayutthaya was considered by European traders to be an ideal place to live. After the siege and ruin of Ayutthaya by the Burmese army, Bangkok became the new "capital" for the Thai people, and it, too, was an enlightened city compared to the squalor of European cities.

Today, the huge metropolis that is Bangkok is a fascinating tangle of traffic and skyscrapers. Navigation in Bangkok is a challenge even for residents. You see, there is no true map of the city; it's far too old a place for that. Most addresses merely describe the street, the side street and then the really small alley of the place you're looking for. This can be frustrating. Of course, the wonderful thing about Bangkok is that you don't have to travel by road; you can also travel by boat. It's very convenient to speed along the river and avoid miles of unnecessary traffic.

Bangkok is a city of light and dark. It has been said that nowhere else can you find so many paradoxes in culture and society than in Bangkok.

There is a place to eat and a type of food to go with just about every aspect of Thai life. One aspect that I find fascinating is the "Palace Cuisine." Royal Thai cuisine is a refined style of

Royal Barge Procession on the Chao Phraya River

45

cooking, previously prepared for noble families only. Over the years it has become easier to find royal-style Thai cuisine at restaurants, but being a cuisine for kings, it is costly to prepare. The chef must not only be a talented cook but a skilled carver as well, as many palace dishes are made with, presented in or surrounded by stunning fruit and vegetable carvings.

Beyond the kitchen, Thailand has much to interest the traveler: historic culture, lively arts, exotic islands, nightlife, a tradition of friendliness and hospitality to strangers – the land of smiles! And if you have the slightest interest in monastic ruins, restored temples and Buddhism, Thailand is the place to go.

The culture of Thailand contains equal amounts of history and exotica and can be quite daunting when you first arrive there. It's hard to beat the excitement (or sometimes, the frustration) of such an encounter. One of the best aspects of this country is that it frequently seems as though little has changed here over the centuries. Especially when you get out of the big city and begin to explore more remote areas, with their regional culinary specialties.

Kinaree at Wat Pra Keo in the grounds of the Grand Palace

THAI STIR-FRIED MUSHROOMS WITH CASHEW NUTS

There's a wonderful restaurant on Dinsao Road in Bangkok, a tiny place serving a variety of vegetarian Thai dishes. I really enjoy this dish the way they prepare it. It's a popular Thai classic normally made with chicken or pork. It's not too spicy and it tastes best served over a mound of freshly cooked jasmine rice. Feel free to add some thin slices of chicken, pork or even seafood if you like.

SEASONING

1 tsp/5 mL salt
¼ tsp/1 mL white pepper
1 tbsp/15 mL fish sauce
¼ cup/60 mL vegetable or
   chicken stock or water
3 cloves garlic, coarsely chopped
2 small green chilies, minced

MAIN INGREDIENTS

3 tbsp/45 mL vegetable oil
2 cans (14 oz/398 mL) straw mushrooms,
   drained and sliced in half
   or ½ lb/250 g fresh mushrooms, sliced
½ cup/125 g raw cashew nuts
2 tsp/10 mL cornstarch dissolved in
   1 tbsp/15 mL water

GARNISH
Sliced green onion

METHOD

1. Combine the salt, white pepper, fish sauce and stock in a small bowl. Prepare all remaining ingredients and have at hand.

2. Preheat a wok over medium-high heat. Add the oil and a moment later add the cashew nuts. Stir-fry the cashews until golden brown. Quickly and carefully remove them from the oil and set aside.

3. Add the garlic and chilies to the hot oil and stir-fry a few seconds while they impart their flavor to the hot oil. Add the mushrooms and stir-fry for 1 to 2 minutes.

4. Add the stock and fish sauce mixture and bring to boil. Return the fried cashews to the wok and stir.

5. Stir the cornstarch and water mixture into the boiling sauce to thicken it. Garnish and serve.

THAI STUFFED OMELETS

 have a lot of fun with this recipe because I always manage to mess up the omelets. They aren't particularly difficult, but if you saw my efforts you might wonder! I'm envious of the street vendors who line up neat rows of perfectly square, stuffed omelets. But don't be dissuaded by my shortcomings. This recipe is tasty enough no matter what your omelet-making skills may be.

SPICE PASTE

2 tsp/10 mL peppercorns
3 to 4 coriander roots
3 cloves garlic, minced
2 tsp/10 mL salt

SEASONING

2 to 4 small green chilies, minced
¼ tsp/1 mL white pepper
½ tsp/2 mL sugar
1 tbsp/15 mL fish sauce

MAIN INGREDIENTS

2 tbsp/30 mL vegetable oil (for the filling)
½ lb/250 g lean minced pork or chicken
4 shallot onions, coarsely chopped
1 small tomato, cubed
1 to 2 tbsp/15 to 30 mL freshly chopped dill,
   mint, coriander or Thai basil
3 to 4 tbsp 45 to 60 mL vegetable oil
   (for the omelets)
4 eggs, beaten with ¼ cup/50 mL water

GARNISH

Lettuce leaves, lime wedges and fresh chilies

METHOD

1. Using a mortar and pestle or a blender or small food processor, pound or grind the spice paste ingredients in the order given until they form a coarse paste. Have all the remaining ingredients prepared and at hand.

2. Preheat a wok or non-stick frying pan over medium-high heat. Add the 2 tbsp/25 mL oil and, a minute later, the spice paste. Fry the spice paste until fragrant and golden brown and then add the minced chilies and stir. Add the minced pork or chicken and continue to fry until almost cooked (when it changes color).

3. Add the chopped shallot onions along with the white pepper, sugar and fish sauce and continue to cook, stirring until the meat begins to brown. Add the tomato and stir gently until heated through. Stir in the chopped herb. Set the filling aside in a bowl and clean out the wok or frying pan. Re-heat the wok or frying pan over medium-high heat.

4. Add about a ¼ of the oil for frying the omelets to the pan, and when the oil is hot add ¼ of the beaten egg mixture to the pan. Tilt the wok to create a thin round omelet. While the omelet is still wet, spoon ¼ of the filling mixture into the center and fold the sides of the omelet over the filling to form a square. Allow the omelet to cook until golden brown. Turn the omelet over onto a plate and cook the remaining three omelets in the same manner.

5. Garnish and serve.

THAI CORN CAKES

In the mid-afternoon, and only in the mid-afternoon, there is a place on the edge of Chinatown, near the Chao Phraya River, where you can buy freshly cooked corn cakes studded with small shrimp and fragrant with coriander root. Like English fish and chips, they are served wrapped in newspaper and accompanied by a sweet vinegary sauce. With a fresh icy glass of lime juice, they are the perfect siesta snack enjoyed under a shady tree. I like them best with a few spoonfuls of coarsely chopped red chilies added to the batter. But be warned: you'll need several glasses of lime juice if you make them that way!

SPICE PASTE

1 tsp/5 mL peppercorns
2 to 3 coriander roots
2 to 3 cloves garlic, minced
1 tbsp/15 mL palm sugar
2 tsp/10 mL salt

SEASONING

2 to 3 tbsp/30 to 45 mL fish sauce

MAIN INGREDIENTS

3 cups/750 mL corn kernels, fresh or frozen
1 lb/500 g small shrimp, coarsely chopped
¼ cup/60 mL cornstarch
½ cup/125 mL flour
4 large eggs, beaten
Vegetable oil for shallow frying

GARNISH

Sprigs of fresh coriander and cucumber
  relish (see recipe, page 105)

METHOD

1. Using a mortar and pestle or a small blender or food processor, pound or grind the spice paste ingredients in the order given until they form a coarse paste. Have all the remaining ingredients prepared and at hand. Preheat oven to 150° F/65° C.

2. Combine the spice paste with the remaining ingredients and seasoning, in the order given (except for the oil), to make a thick batter.

3. In a large, deep frying pan, heat enough oil for shallow frying (about 1 in/2.5 cm deep). When the oil is hot, begin frying the batter by the tablespoonful, cooking no more than 3 to 5 corn cakes at a time. Turn the corn cakes over as they brown on each side. When the cakes are golden brown on both sides, use a slotted spoon to transfer them to a plate lined with paper towel. Keep them warm in the oven.

4. Serve the corn cakes warm, garnished with fresh coriander and accompanied by cucumber relish.

FRESH OR FROZEN?

You can use either fresh or frozen corn in this recipe. If you use frozen kernels, be sure they are thoroughly defrosted and very well drained. You may need to roll them loosely in paper towels to absorb the excess moisture.

TOM YUM SOUP

This soup is very popular in Thailand with Thais and tourists alike. It's not unusual to have this soup accompanied by just a bowl of plain jasmine rice for breakfast, lunch or as a very late night snack. The name for this dish describes two of the oldest cooking techniques in the Thai kitchen: *tom* means a dish that is boiled or simmered and *yum* (or *yam*) is a term traditionally used to describe mixed dishes or salads. In its modern sense it means a dish made with chilies, lime juice and fish sauce.

SEASONING

2 stalks lemon grass trimmed
   cut into 2-inch/5-cm pieces
5 to 8 thick slices of fresh galanga
3 to 6 fresh kaffir lime leaves
Fresh chilies to taste,
   sliced in half lengthwise
2 to 3 tsp/10 to 15 mL
Thai roasted chili paste (optional)
2 to 3 dashes of fish sauce, or to taste
3 tbsp/45 mL fresh lime juice, or to taste

MAIN INGREDIENTS

5 to 6 cups/1.2 to 1.5 L chicken stock
15 straw mushrooms or other mushroom
   of your choice, cleaned, trimmed of
   stems and cut in half
15 large prawns, peeled with tails on,
   or 1 lb/500 g thinly sliced meat or
   seafood of your choice

GARNISH

Fresh coriander leaves and lime wedges

METHOD

1. Prepare all ingredients and have at hand. In a deep pan bring the stock to a boil. Adjust the heat to a low boil and add the lemon grass, galanga, lime leaves and chilies. Allow the soup to simmer for 3 to 5 minutes.

2. Add the roasted chili paste (if using), fish sauce and lime juice and stir to dissolve the chili paste. Add the mushroom halves followed by the prawns (or sliced meat or seafood) and stir.

3. Taste the soup and adjust the seasoning, adding more fish sauce, lime juice and a pinch of sugar as desired.

4. As soon as the prawns are cooked to your liking, serve the soup garnished with fresh coriander. Pass the lime wedges around at the table.

THAI CHICKEN SOUP WITH COCONUT MILK

his soup is very elegant as well as being very easy to prepare. A beautiful creamy white broth redolent of lime leaf and galanga, it should be served in your finest soup plates or bowls as a memorable beginning to any meal. Be sure to simmer the soup only (do not boil) after you add the thick coconut cream or it will appear oily.

SEASONING

1 stalk lemon grass, trimmed
  and cut into 2-inch/5-cm pieces
6 to 7 thick slices of fresh galanga
3 to 4 fresh kaffir lime leaves
2 to 4 small fresh chilies,
  sliced in half lengthwise
1 to 2 tbsp/15 to 30 mL
  fish sauce, or to taste
1 to 2 tbsp/15 to 30 mL
  fresh lime juice, or to taste
1 tsp/5 mL sugar
1 tsp/5mL salt

MAIN INGREDIENTS

3 cups/750 mL chicken stock
½ lb/250 g boneless chicken breast,
  thinly sliced
2 14-oz/400-mL cans of coconut milk,
  separated

GARNISH
Your choice of fresh herbs

METHOD

1. Prepare all ingredients and have at hand. In a deep pan, bring the stock to a boil. Adjust the heat to a low boil and add the lemon grass, galanga, lime leaves and chilies. Allow the soup to simmer for 3 to 5 minutes.

2. Add the thin coconut milk, fish sauce, lime juice, sugar and salt and stir. Bring the soup just to a boil and add the chicken. Allow the soup to return to a low boil until the chicken is thoroughly cooked.

3. Stir in the thick coconut cream and taste the soup, adjusting the seasoning by adding more fish sauce, lime juice or a pinch of sugar as desired.

4. Garnish and serve.

THAI PORK AND TOFU SOUP

The spice paste of peppercorns, coriander root and garlic is one of the fundamentals of the Thai hawker's repertoire — a mixture of traditional Thai aromatics without any New World influences, notably chilies. The other ingredients in this dish are fundamentally Chinese, and the fresh tofu, dried mushrooms, lily buds and mung bean noodles are classic Cantonese soup garnishes. This recipe is a good example of how the Thai can work their magic on an old favorite from another culture. The soup is soothing and healthful — ideal as a light, hot-weather lunch or as a great side dish.

SPICE PASTE

2 tsp/10 mL peppercorns
3 to 4 coriander roots
3 cloves garlic, minced
2 tsp/10 mL salt

MAIN INGREDIENTS

5 to 6 cups/1.25 to 1.5 L chicken stock
½ lb/250 g lean minced pork
4 to 5 dried Chinese mushrooms,
    soaked for 15-20 minutes, drained and
    trimmed of stems
8 dried lily buds, soaked for 15 minutes,
    drained and tied in a knot
2 green onions,
    cut in 1-inch/2.5-cm sections
1 block fresh tofu, cubed
1 small bundle mung bean noodles,
    soaked for 15 minutes and drained
Salt, sugar and fish sauce to taste

GARNISH
Fresh sprigs of coriander

METHOD

1. Prepare all ingredients and have at hand. Using a mortar and pestle or a small blender or food processor, pound or grind the spice paste ingredients in the order given until they form a coarse paste.

2. Add the spice paste to the minced pork and mix thoroughly. Form the mixture into small balls, no bigger than walnuts, and set aside.

3. In a deep pan, bring the stock to boil. Drop the pork balls into the boiling stock and cook until they change color and begin to float.

4. Adjust the heat to a slow simmer and add the Chinese mushrooms, lily buds and green onions. Simmer for 3 minutes.

5. Add the tofu cubes and bean threads and stir gently. Taste the soup and adjust seasoning, adding salt, sugar or fish sauce as desired.

6. Garnish and serve.

GRILLED PRAWN SOUP

The Thai name for this soup, *Tom Kloang Goong Yang*, gives away its ancient lineage. *Kloang* is an old Thai word referring to a soup made with grilled vegetables and seafood. The fact that this soup is made with water instead of stock is a further indication that this is original Thai cuisine. When preparing this dish, if you prefer you can dry roast the garlic, shallots and chilies in a non-stick frying pan over medium-high heat.

SPICE PASTE

2 tsp/10 mL peppercorns
3 to 4 coriander roots
3 cloves garlic, minced
2 tsp/10 mL salt

SEASONING

7 shallot onions
5 cloves of garlic
3 large dried red chilies
3 thick slices of fresh galanga
2 - 6 inch/15 cm long pieces
    lemon grass, bruised
3 to 4 tbsp/45 to 60 mL fish sauce
3 to 4 tbsp/45 to 60 mL fresh lime juice
1 to 2 tbsp/15 to 30 mL tamarind water

MAIN INGREDIENTS

5 cups/1250 ml boiling water
1 cup/250 mL grilled prawns, halved
    lengthwise (see sidebar)

GARNISH

Sprigs of fresh coriander and Thai basil

METHOD

1. Preheat a grill or small barbecue while you prepare the spice paste.

2. Using a mortar and pestle, or a small blender or food processor, pound or grind the spice paste ingredients in the order given until they form a coarse paste. Prepare all remaining ingredients and have at hand.

3. Thread the shallot onions and garlic onto wooden skewers so that no wood is visible. Grill the shallots and garlic slowly until browned all over. Remove the garlic and shallots from the skewers and cut the shallots in half.

4. Grill the dried chilies until they soften and change color. Do not allow them to burn. Split them open and remove the seeds and ribs.

5. Add the spice paste, shallots, garlic, chilies, galanga and lemon grass to the water. Simmer for 5 minutes.

6. Add the fish sauce, lime juice, tamarind water and grilled prawns. Taste and adjust seasoning by adding sugar, salt, fresh lime juice or fish sauce as desired.

7. Garnish and serve.

GRILLING PRAWNS

Lay 2 or 3 pieces of aluminum foil (12 x 16 inch/30 x 40 cm each), shiny side up, on top of each other. (Use 2 pieces if you are grilling on a gas element; 3 if on an electric element.) Fold the layers in half to make a rectangle, and then unfold. Toss the prawns with oil and lay them no more than 2 deep on one side of the foil. Fold the other half of the foil over the prawns and fold the edges to seal the packet well. Place the packet directly over an element set on medium-high heat. The packet should begin to sizzle and puff up almost immediately. Grill the prawns 60 to 90 seconds per side. (Use a pair of kitchen tongs to turn the packet over without piercing it.) Turn off the heat and set the packet on a plate. Using scissors, open the packet, being careful not to let the steam scald you. The prawns should be firm to the touch, cooked through and bright pink.

Wat Arun, Temple of the Dawn, at sunset

CUCUMBER SALAD

 his salad bursts with fresh flavors. It is particularly delicious with grilled foods and is popular at pot lucks. Be sure to add the peanuts at the last moment so they remain crunchy. You can also try substituting other crisp, sweet vegetables or fruits for the cucumber. You'll be pleased with the results.

SEASONING

2 tbsp/30 mL fish sauce
¼ cup/60 mL fresh lime juice
2 to 3 tsp/10 to 15 mL sugar
2 shallot onions, thinly sliced
1 to 2 green onions, finely sliced
2 tbsp/30 mL coarsely chopped mint
1 tbsp/15 mL coarsely chopped
   fresh coriander
2 small red chilies, thinly sliced
2 to 3 tbsp/30 mL to 45 mL ground,
   dried shrimp

MAIN INGREDIENTS

1 English cucumber, seeded and
   cubed in bite-size pieces
Salt
GARNISH
Lettuce leaves, crushed roasted peanuts and
   Thai roasted chili flakes; lime wedges on
   the side

METHOD

1. Lightly salt the cucumber and allow to drain in a colander for about 30 minutes.

2. Use a mortar and pestle or a small blender or food processor to pound the dried shrimp into a coarse floss. Measure 2 tbsp/30 mL of this shrimp floss and set aside. Meanwhile make sure all the remaining ingredients are prepared and at hand.

3. Combine the fish sauce, lime juice and sugar, stirring well until the sugar dissolves. Add the shallot onions, green onions, mint, coriander and chilies. Set aside while you complete the recipe.

4. Drain the cucumber well, rolling it loosely in paper towel if the pieces are very wet. Place the cucumber in a non-reactive bowl and add the fish sauce mixture and the ground, dried shrimp.

5. Gently toss the salad and serve on the lettuce leaves, garnished with the crushed roasted peanuts, chili flakes and lime wedges.

right: An assortment of Thai vegetables
for salads and soups

THAI GREEN PAPAYA SALAD

In the northern Thai city of Chiang Mai, people are passionate about this addictive, fantastic and fiery salad from Laos, known as *Som Tam*. Fortunately, everybody knows where the best som tam can be found; unfortunately, no one can agree which place that is. This is an awesome accompaniment to any grilled or roast meat, fish or poultry.

SEASONING

1 to 3 fresh chilies
3 to 4 cloves garlic
3 to 4 tbsp/45 to 60 mL fresh lime juice
2 to 3 tbsp/30 to 45 mL fish sauce
1 tbsp/15 mL sugar

MAIN INGREDIENTS

1 green papaya,
    about 1 ¾ to 2 lb/700 g to 1 kg,
    peeled, seeded and grated
1 large carrot, peeled and grated
¼ lb/125 g green beans,
    trimmed and cut into 1-in/2.5 cm pieces
2 tomatoes, diced

GARNISH

2 tbsp/30 mL roasted peanuts,
    coarsely chopped
1 to 2 tbsp/15 to 30 mL ground
    dried shrimp

METHOD

1. Prepare all ingredients and have at hand. In a mortar and pestle pound the chilies and garlic into a rough paste. Add some of the green beans and bruise them with the pestle. Add more beans and pound them lightly to mix them with the garlic and chilies. Transfer the bean-chili mixture and remaining green beans to a non-reactive bowl. Add the green papaya and mix well. Using the pestle, gently bruise the papaya-bean mixture.

2. Combine the fresh lime juice, fish sauce and sugar and stir well until the sugar dissolves. Combine with the green bean mixture and add the carrot and tomatoes. Toss well.

3. Taste and adjust the seasoning, adding more lime juice, fish sauce or sugar as desired. Garnish and serve.

*left: Bangkok's Chinatown at night,
an exciting place to shop & eat*

CHINESE BROCCOLI AND PRAWN SALAD

I have enjoyed this wonderfully refreshing salad many times in Phuket. Made with Chinese broccoli and plump juicy prawns, the Thai call it *Yam Pak Ka-na*, indicating how it is made and what it contains. *Yam* is one of the oldest Thai cooking techniques. The best way to think of the term is as a fresh dish involving little or no cooking that is seasoned with lime juice, fish sauce and chilies and possibly shallot onions, lemon grass and fresh herbs. *Pak ka-na* is Thai for Chinese broccoli, which you may recognize as gai lan from Cantonese restaurant menus.

SEASONING

2 tbsp/30 mL fish sauce
4 tbsp/60 mL fresh lime juice
2 to 3 tsp/10 to 15 mL sugar
3 to 4 shallot onions, thinly sliced
2 tbsp/30 mL lemon grass,
   very thinly sliced
1 to 2 tbsp/15 to 30 mL green onion, sliced
1 tbsp/15 mL mint, coarsely chopped
2 tbsp/30 mL fresh coriander,
   coarsely chopped
2 small red chilis, thinly sliced

MAIN INGREDIENTS

5 cups/1.25 L boiling water
3 stalks Chinese broccoli (gai lan), trimmed
   and cut into bite-size pieces
15 large prawns, peeled with tails on

GARNISH

Coarsely chopped fresh coriander and
   thinly sliced red chilis to sprinkle on
   top; lime wedges on the side

METHOD

1. Have all ingredients prepared and at hand. Combine the fish sauce, lime juice and sugar and stir well until the sugar dissolves. Add the shallot onion, lemon grass, green onion, mint, coriander and chilis. Set this mixture aside while you complete the recipe.

2. In a large deep pot blanch the gai lan in the boiling water until bright green (3 to 4 minutes). Using a large strainer, scoop the gai lan from the boiling water and chill it in a large, deep bowl half-filled with ice water.

3. Drain the gai lan well and place into a non-reactive bowl.

4. Quickly cook the large prawns in the boiling water and chill them in the same manner as the gai lan. Add the cooked prawns to the gai lan in the non-reactive bowl and add the dressing from step one.

5. Gently toss the salad and serve garnished.

THAI GRILLED PRAWN SALAD

This dish is wicked fun for entertaining. I like to get all the ingredients organized ahead of time and then put it all together with friends while having a drink before dinner in the kitchen. Try it some time; you'll be famous in your own home!

SEASONING

2 tbsp/30 mL fish sauce
5 tbsp/75 mL fresh lime juice
2 tsp/10 mL sugar
3 shallot onions, thinly sliced
2 stalks of lemon grass, very thinly sliced
2 red chilies, thinly sliced

MAIN INGREDIENTS

1 ripe papaya, peeled, seeded and cubed
1 tbsp/15 mL fresh mint, coarsely chopped
1 tbsp/15 mL fresh coriander, coarsely chopped
1 lb/500 g medium-size prawns, peeled with tails on
2 tsp/10 mL salt
1 tbsp/15 mL oil

GARNISH

Crushed roasted peanuts, coarsely chopped green onion, fresh coriander and thinly sliced red chilies

METHOD

1. Prepare all ingredients and have at hand. Toss the prawns with the salt and allow them to sit for 10 minutes while you make the seasoning.

2. Combine the fish sauce, lime juice, sugar, shallot onions, lemon grass and chilies. Stir well until the sugar dissolves.

3. Grill the prawns (see sidebar on page 61 for instructions for grilling).

4. Pour the grilled prawns and any juices into a non-reactive bowl. Add the papaya, mint, coriander and the fish sauce mixture.

5. Gently toss the salad. Garnish and serve.

THAI PINEAPPLE RICE

I laughed when somebody once described this dish as the typical Thai birthday cake. I had a hard time imagining people singing "Happy Birthday" while gathered around a stuffed pineapple. But if you do go to Thailand, more than once you will see a smiling group of people doing just that. The Thai name for this dish is *Khao Pad Sapparod*, which means, literally, rice stir fried with pineapple. The seasoning of coriander root, fish sauce and coconut milk can be prepared ahead of time and even frozen for future use.

right: *An offering of foods to family ancestors during a Tamboon Kraduk ceremony*

SEASONING

2 tbsp/30 mL chopped coriander root
½ tsp/2 mL white pepper
¼ cup/60 mL sugar
¼ cup/60 mL fish sauce
1 ½ cup/375 mL coconut milk

MAIN INGREDIENTS

2 to 3 tbsp/30 to 45 mL vegetable oil
4 cups/1 L freshly cooked rice
½ cup/125 mL roasted cashews
1 pineapple
½ to 1 cup cooked shrimp, Chinese
   barbecue pork or other leftover cooked
   meat cut into bite-size pieces (optional)

GARNISH

Coarsely chopped green onion

METHOD

1. Using a sharp knife, cut off one third of the pineapple, lengthwise and carefully carve out the fruit to form a boat-like container for the finished dish. Cut half the fruit into cubes. Reserve the remainder for another use. If the fronds of the pineapple are large, trim them with a pair of kitchen scissors. Prepare all remaining ingredients and have at hand.

2. In a small saucepan, heat the coconut milk to a boil. Add the coriander root, white pepper, sugar and fish sauce. Reduce heat and simmer the sauce for 3 to 5 minutes, then strain.

3. Preheat a wok over medium-high heat and add the oil, to coat the sides of the wok. When the oil is hot, add the meat, pineapple, cashews and rice. Stir and toss to combine well.

4. Slowly pour the seasoned coconut milk over the rice, ¼ cup/60 mL at a time until the rice is just moistened. You will have more than enough seasoned coconut milk; any leftover can be frozen for future use. Continue stir-frying until the rice is heated through.

5. Fill the pineapple with the hot rice mixture. Garnish and serve.

THAI FRIED RICE NOODLES

I t was the Chinese who introduced stir-fried rice noodle dishes to Southeast Asia. As a result, there are many regions with their own variations. This recipe might be more familiar as Pad Thai, an item you will find on any Thai restaurant menu. The authentic name is *Gwitdeow Pad Thai. Gwitdeow* is a Chinese term common to many Southeast Asian languages for rice noodle. *Pad Thai* means stir-fried, Thai style.

SEASONING

3 cloves garlic, minced
2 tsp/10 mL chili flakes
2 to 3 tbsp/30 to 45 mL fish sauce
1 tbsp/15 mL rice vinegar
2 tsp/10 mL sugar
1 to 2 tbsp/15 to 30 mL tamarind water

MAIN INGREDIENTS

8 oz/250 g dry, narrow rice noodles
3 to 4 tbsp vegetable oil
5 large raw prawns, peeled and cut in half
¼ lb/125 g minced lean pork
2 pieces deep fried tofu, or tofu puffs,
   cubed (about ½ cup/125 mL)
1 to 2 tbsp vegetable oil
2 large eggs, beaten
1 cup bean sprouts, trimmed

GARNISH

2 tbsp/30 mL roasted peanuts,
   coarsely chopped
1 to 2 tbsp/15 to 30 mL ground
   dried shrimp
Coarsely chopped green onion and fresh
   coriander; thinly sliced red chilies.

above: Phuket noodle vendor in action

METHOD

1. Soak the rice noodles in hot water for 10 to 15 minutes or until soft. Meanwhile, prepare all remaining ingredients and have at hand.

2. Drain the noodles well and set-aside.

3. In a small bowl, combine fish sauce, vinegar, sugar and tamarind water. Stir well to dissolve the sugar. Set aside.

4. Preheat a wok or large, deep frying pan over medium-high to high heat. Add the 3 to 4 tbsp/45 to 60 mL oil and as soon as it is hot add the garlic and chili flakes. Stir once and add the prawns. Keep stirring until the prawns begin to change color and then add the pork. Keep cooking until the pork changes color and then add the tofu.

5. Add the fish sauce mixture and bring to a boil. Add the rice noodles and stir well, tossing to combine with the sauce. Continue to cook until the noodles become soft. Transfer the noodles to a serving platter.

6. Return the pan to the heat and add the remaining 1 to 2 tbsp/15 to 30 mL oil. Add the eggs to the pan and allow them to cook for a few seconds without stirring. Stir the eggs and add the bean sprouts. Continue to cook until the eggs are almost firm. Return the noodles to the pan and stir to mix the eggs, sprouts and noodles.

7. Return the noodles to the serving platter, garnish and serve.

THAI FRIED RICE WITH PORK

My friends in Bangkok love to go out to a jazz club or disco for a night on the town. Sometimes I think they like to spend so much energy just to work up an appetite. Late at night, snacks on the streets of Bangkok are different from the evening ones, which are different from the afternoon ones, and so on. When I'm hungry late at night, I search out a hawker who will make me a plate of fried rice with pork accompanied by crisp, fresh cucumber, chunky wedges of ripe tomato and topped with a fried egg. Like the Thais around me, I dress it up with roasted chili flakes, a squeeze of fresh lime juice and a sprinkle of sugar. After a night of jazz clubs and discos the silence around me seems strange; the food is so good, no one speaks until the plates are empty.

SEASONING

2 tbsp/30 mL minced garlic
1 to 2 tbsp/15 to 30 mL fish sauce
2 tsp/10 mL freshly ground black pepper

MAIN INGREDIENTS

3 tbsp/45 mL vegetable oil
½ to ¾ lb/250 to 375 g lean minced pork
⅓ cup/75 mL snow peas, sliced
    ½-inch/2.5 cm long on the diagonal
3 to 5 cups/750 to 1250 mL leftover
    cooked rice, grains separated
4 large eggs
Salt, sugar, and pepper to taste

GARNISH

Fresh lettuce leaves, slices of cucumber,
    tomato wedges, sprigs of fresh coriander
    and wedges of lime

METHOD

1. Prepare all ingredients and have at hand.

2. Heat a wok or large frying pan over high heat and add the oil. As soon as the oil begins to form a haze, add the minced garlic. When the garlic turns golden, add the minced pork. Stir-fry the pork until it is cooked through and begins to brown.

3. Add the snow peas and fry until they turn bright green. Add the fish sauce and pepper and stir.

4. Add the rice and stir-fry until heated through. Taste the mixture and adjust the seasoning by adding salt, sugar, fish sauce or ground pepper as desired. Turn off the heat. Keep the rice warm while you fry the 4 eggs sunny side up.

5. Serve the fried rice on individual plates with a fried egg and other garnish.

right: Temple of the Dawn, Thailand

FRESH NOODLES WITH ROAST PORK

There is a funky guest house run by a friend of mine not far from the Democracy Monument on the edge of old Bangkok. It's a comfortable old teak home, not a hostel, and you have to fend for yourself for meals. Just down the alley and around the corner is Tanon Dinsao, a popular street lined with hawkers offering all kinds of breakfast fare. The best deal is at a modest Chinese-Thai restaurant called Tien Zhong that will serve you a bowl of freshly cooked noodles topped with barbecued pork and a wedge of bright green Shanghai bok choy. In the tropical heat this is the perfect breakfast: light and nutritious with protein and fiber. The secret in this version is a sprinkling of crisply fried garlic, light soy and sugar over the noodles before anything else is added. This recipe can be made with any tender, quick-cooking vegetable in place of the bok choy.

SEASONING

For the stock:
2 tbsp/30 mL fish sauce
Salt, sugar and white pepper to taste

For the noodles:
2 tbsp/30 mL crisply fried garlic
2 tbsp/30 mL light soy sauce
Sugar, pinch

MAIN INGREDIENTS

½ lb/250 g Chinese barbecued pork
¾ to 1 lb/375 to 500 g fresh egg noodles
8 cups/2 L boiling water
4 to 5 cups/1 to 1.25 L chicken stock
2 small Shanghai bok choy, quartered
    lengthwise and cleaned

GARNISH
Coarsely chopped green onion, fresh
    coriander, thinly sliced red chilies and
    crushed roasted peanuts

METHOD

1. Prepare all ingredients and have at hand. Heat the chicken stock to a simmer in a medium-sized pan over medium heat. Meanwhile cook the noodles in the boiling water until just done (3 to 4 minutes).

2. While the noodles are cooking and in the same water, quickly cook the Shanghai bok choy until bright green (2 to 3 minutes). Retrieve the bok choy from the boiling noodles and rinse them well with cold running water. Set aside.

3. Rinse the noodles under cold, running water. Drain them very well and place them in a bowl. Toss the cooked noodles with the noodle seasoning and divide them among 4 to 6 serving bowls.

4. Add the stock seasoning to the simmering chicken stock. Add the barbecued pork. Adjust the heat to maintain the simmer.

5. Remove the barbecued pork from the stock and arrange the slices on top of the noodles. Tuck in a piece of bok choy. Garnish each bowl with the green onion, coriander and ground peanuts. Serve each bowl of noodles with a smaller bowl of the broth on the side.

MEAT SATAYS

The dark of the Southeast Asian night is punctuated by the bright fires of the satay vendors. In fact, the dark of the night in many Southeast Asian cities is lit by these grinning maniacs, frantically fanning the flames and aromas of their charcoals grills. This Thai version is very simple to prepare and gives you a real taste of what Bangkok snacking is all about. The marinade is, of course, multi-purpose. Use it to flavor chops, steaks, roasts and meats for stir-frying.

SEASONING

2 cloves garlic, minced
2 tsp/10 mL ground turmeric
1 tsp/5 mL ground coriander
½ tsp/2 mL cumin
1 tbsp/15 mL sugar
1 tbsp/15 mL fish sauce
Salt, pinch
¼ cup/50 mL vegetable oil

MAIN INGREDIENTS

1 ¼ lb/600 g lean beef, chicken, lamb or
  pork, thinly sliced into strips

GARNISH

Tomato and cucumber, peeled small shallot
onions and lettuce leaves

METHOD

1. Soak a package of small bamboo skewers in water for 2 to 3 hours. Prepare all ingredients and have at hand.

2. Combine the seasoning ingredients in a medium-size stainless steel or glass bowl and mix well. Mix the meat with the seasoning and marinate at room temperature for one hour or refrigerate overnight.

3. Preheat a grill or broiler. Thread the marinated meat onto the skewers. Cook the satays over a hot fire or broil them in the oven 3 to 5 minutes per side, or until done. Do not leave them unattended! Serve immediately on a garnished plate. Ideally, satay should also be accompanied by peanut sauce (page 105) and cucumber relish (page 105).

BROILING SKEWERS

The best flavor comes from grilling, but you can broil skewers in the oven, too. Use a cookie sheet lined with aluminum foil and a cake rack to keep the skewers off the foil, otherwise they will simmer in their own juices, becoming tough and dry.

above: *Fish sauce, the all-purpose seasoning in Southeast Asia*

PENANG BEEF CURRY

Penang has always been a crossroads for many different cuisines and cultures. The cuisine reflects Thai, Chinese, Indian and Western colonial influences. This is a popular recipe for a Muslim-influenced Thai curry in the Penang style. *Penang Nuea*, as the Thai call it, is so popular it can be found all over Thailand. It's a great example of what is known as a dry curry. The sauce is reduced to coat the pieces of meat and intensify the flavor.

SEASONING

2 - 3-inch/8-cm pieces of lemon grass
1 to 2 tbsp/15 to 30 mL Thai red curry
    paste or Penang curry paste

MAIN INGREDIENTS

Cream from 1 can (14 oz/400 mL size)
    coconut milk
2 to 3 tsp/10 to 15 mL fish sauce,
    or to taste
Sugar, pinch
Black pepper, pinch
½ to ¾ lb/250 to 375 g lean tender beef,
    cut in small thick slices
2 tbsp/30 mL crushed roasted peanuts

GARNISH

Fresh Thai basil leaves and thinly sliced
    red chilies

METHOD

1. Prepare all ingredients and have at hand. Preheat a non-stick frying pan over medium-high heat.

2. Add 3 to 4 tbsp/45 to 60 mL of the coconut cream to the frying pan and reduce it by boiling vigorously and stirring until the cream separates (this can take a few minutes). Do not allow the reducing cream to burn.

3. Add the lemon grass and the curry paste and stir well so that the coconut oil absorbs the aromatic oils from the curry paste and lemon grass.

4. Add the beef and fry it with the curry paste until it changes color on all sides. Do not over-stir. Let the pieces sizzle for a moment on a side, then stir to color the other side. (The meat does not need to brown, but the sugars from the coconut cream will brown. Be careful not to let the sugars burn.)

5. Add the remaining coconut cream, the crushed peanuts, a dash of fish sauce and a pinch each of sugar and black pepper. Bring the sauce to a gentle boil for 3 to 4 minutes or until the beef is cooked to your liking and the sauce is thick and coating the pieces of meat. Control the heat to avoid burning the sauce.

6. Taste the sauce before the cooking is done and adjust seasoning, adding more sugar or fish sauce as desired.

7. Garnish and serve.

CHICKEN IN THAI GREEN CURRY

Perhaps the best way to think of curry is as a sauce to go with rice, so wherever you find rice as a staple, you'll probably find a type of curry, too. The Thai approach to making curry was influenced by (and maybe originated from) the curries of Sri Lanka during the 16th century. It was then that Thai chefs began to use coconut milk for savory dishes. When Thai royalty converted to Sri Lankan Buddhism it would seem that trade in matters both spiritual and culinary benefited the two nations.

right: Prepared market foods, Thailand

SEASONING

1 to 3 tbsp/15 to 45 mL Thai green curry paste

MAIN INGREDIENTS

2 - 14 oz/400 mL cans coconut milk, separated
3 fresh lime leaves 2 to 4 fresh green or red chilies, cut in half lengthwise (optional)
1 lb/500 grams chicken, white or dark meat, boneless or bone in, cut into bite-size pieces
1 to 2 cups/250 to 500 mL vegetables of your choice, cut into bite-size pieces
1 to 2 tbsp/15 to 30 mL fish sauce to taste.
Sugar and salt to taste
Leaves from 2 or more sprigs of Thai basil

GARNISH

A dollop of thick coconut cream, flowers and sprigs of Thai basil and diagonal slices of fresh green or red chilies on top.

METHOD

1. Prepare all the ingredients and have at hand.

2. Heat a non-reactive, heavy bottomed deep pan over medium heat. Add 3 or 4 generous spoonfuls of the coconut cream and cook, stirring until reduced and the coconut oil begins to separate. Some browning may occur.

3. Add the lime leaves and chilies and stir for ½ a minute. Add the curry paste. Cook until fragrant and well mixed, about 1 minute.

4. Add the chicken pieces to the pan and stir well to coat with the frying paste. Continue to cook to allow the flavors to penetrate the chicken. Do not allow the paste to scorch.

5. Add the thin coconut milk, the remaining rich coconut cream (reserving a dollop for garnish), the fish sauce and a pinch of sugar and of salt. Stir and bring to a boil. Lower heat to a simmer and cook uncovered for 15 minutes. (At this point, the curry can be cooled and refrigerated, or frozen for later use.)

6. Start adding the vegetables that require the longest cooking, so that, when you finish, all the vegetables will be evenly cooked and look their best.

7. Taste and adjust by adding sugar, fish sauce, chilies or salt as desired. Stir in the basil leaves. Garnish and serve.

TWICE-COOKED CHICKEN AND NOODLES

This is a wonderful Thai hawker dish that has its roots in the traditional Chinese kitchen. Twice-cooking, or double-cooking, has many variations, usually combining deep-frying or roasting with a moist cooking technique, such as steaming. Of course, you can change the order of the two techniques and steam before deep-frying, for instance. Double-cooking can be used to change the texture, flavor or appearance of an ingredient to make the dish more pleasing. Here, the goal of double-cooking is to improve the flavor and to break up the preparation of the recipe into two easy-to-manage steps.

SPICE PASTE

2 tsp/10 mL peppercorns
3 to 4 coriander roots
3 cloves garlic, minced
2 tsp/10 mL salt

SEASONING

For the chicken:
2 tbsp/30 mL Chinese wine, or whiskey
2 tbsp/30 mL oyster sauce
2 tsp/10 mL sugar

For the stock:
2 tbsp/30 mL light soy sauce
1 tbsp/15 mL dark soy sauce
1 tbsp/15 mL Worcestershire sauce
Salt, sugar and white pepper to taste

For the noodles:
2 tbsp/30 mL crisply fried garlic
2 tbsp/30 mL light soy sauce

MAIN INGREDIENTS

4 chicken breasts
3 cups/750 ml chicken stock
Vegetable oil (enough for shallow frying)
1 lb/500 g fresh egg noodles
8 cups/2 L boiling water
4 small leaves lettuce

GARNISH

Coarsely chopped green onion, fresh coriander
  and freshly ground sliced red chilies

METHOD

1. Prepare all ingredients and have at hand. Using a mortar and pestle or small blender or food processor, pound or grind the spice paste ingredients in the order given until they form a coarse paste. Combine the spice paste and the seasoning ingredients for the chicken and mix well. Marinate the chicken breasts in this mixture for least 1 hour.

2. Heat the chicken stock to a simmer in a medium-size pan over medium heat.

3. Preheat a wok or pan suitable for shallow frying and add the oil . When the oil is hot, fry the chicken until just golden brown, not cooked through. Remove the chicken and drain.

4. Add the seasonings for the stock to the simmering chicken stock, then add the chicken. Bring the stock to a boil. Lower heat to simmer. Gently cook the chicken until done, about 15 minutes.

5. In a large pan cook the egg noodles in boiling water until just done (3 to 4 minutes from the time the water returns to a boil). Drain and quickly rinse them well with cold, running water. Drain well again and place in a bowl. Toss with the seasonings for the noodles and then divide among 4 to 6 serving bowls.

6. Remove the chicken from the stock and cut each breast into bite-size slices. Arrange the chicken pieces on top of the noodles and tuck in a lettuce leaf. Spoon ¼ cup/50 mL of the stock over the chicken and noodles and garnish each bowl.

THAI BARBECUED CHICKEN

One day, I jumped on board the Bangkok express river taxi with the idea of visiting some friends. Seeing a familiar landmark, I confidently asked for the next stop. But seen from the river and the few canals that remain open to boat traffic, Bangkok is a very different city, and I soon found myself lost with only an idea of the general direction I should take. I tried some promising-looking side streets, following a delicious aroma that led me to the most amazing charcoal grilled chicken I have ever eaten. I bought a whole one for good luck, and I eventually found where I wanted to go.

SPICE PASTE

2 tsp/10 mL peppercorns
¼ to ½ tsp/1 to 2 mL cumin seeds
2 tsp/10 mL coarse salt
1 tbsp/15 mL coarsely chopped coriander root
1-inch/2.5-cm piece fresh turmeric root,
    or 1 tsp/5 mL turmeric powder
1 shallot onion, minced
7 cloves garlic, mashed

SEASONING

2 tsp/10 mL palm sugar or brown sugar
2 tbsp/30 mL fish sauce
Fresh juice of 1 lime
3 tbsp/45 mL vegetable oil

MAIN INGREDIENTS

1 medium chicken split down the back,
    or 1 to 2 lbs/500 g to 1 kg thighs

METHOD

1. Prepare all ingredients and have at hand. Using a mortar and pestle or a small blender or food processor, pound or grind the spice paste ingredients in the order given until they form a coarse paste. Combine the spice paste with the seasoning ingredients and mix well.

2. Open the chicken so that it lays flat. Trim away any loose skin or fat and cut off the wing tips. Marinate the chicken in the spice paste/seasoning mixture in a non-reactive dish for 2 hours or overnight.

3. Preheat a grill or barbecue. Grill the chicken over a medium fire until done (35 to 40 minutes). Alternatively, you can roast the chicken in a 375°F/190°C oven until done, (about 1 hour). Allow the chicken to rest on a platter for 10 minutes before serving

THAI BIRYANI

The Muslim influence throughout Southeast Asia is often overlooked when it comes to regional cuisines. I have enjoyed variations on this dish in the Muslim and Indian neighborhoods in and around Bangkok. The Persians and Arabs also have their own versions of this dish in which succulent pieces of meat are typically cooked layered with saffron-tinted rice. This recipe is not overly complicated, and it can be completed in several easy-to-handle steps. The result is a small feast worthy of a special occasion.

SPICE MIX

For the chicken and the rice:
1 tbsp/15 mL Thai chili flakes
1 ½ tsp/7 mL pepper
2 tsp/10 mL coriander powder
1 tsp/5 mL cumin powder
1 tsp/5 mL turmeric powder
1 tbsp/15 mL salt

For marinating the chicken:
2 tbsp/30 mL ginger, finely minced
2 tbsp/30 mL garlic, finely minced
2 large shallot onions, finely minced
6 tbsp/90 mL plain yogurt

SEASONING

4 green cardamom pods
3 cloves
2-inch/5 cm cinnamon stick
Pinch saffron in 3 cups/750 mL
   very hot water

MAIN INGREDIENTS

6 chicken thighs, skinned
2 tbsp/30 mL butter
5 cups/1.25 L rice
6 cups/1.5 L water
3 tbsp/45 mL vegetable oil
3 tbsp/45 mL salt

For the condiment:
2 small red chilies, sliced
2 small green chilies, sliced
¼ cup/60 mL palm sugar
4 tsp/20 mL white sugar
2 tsp/10 mL salt
1 cup/250 mL vinegar

METHOD

1. Combine the spice mix ingredients for the chicken and rice and set aside. Preheat an oven to 350°F/180°C. Prepare all remaining ingredients and have at hand.

2. In a medium-size bowl, combine the ginger, garlic, shallot onions and 1 tbsp/15 mL of the spice mix. Add the yogurt. Marinate the chicken thighs in this mixture for 1 hour.

3. While the chicken marinates, combine the rice, water, oil and 3 tbsp/45 mL salt in a heavy, deep pot. Bring to a boil, turn down the heat and cook the rice, covered, until the water is absorbed (about 15 minutes). Gently separate the grains of rice with a fork. Cover the rice to keep it hot while you complete the recipe.

4. In a heavy, deep frying pan or casserole with a lid, melt the butter over medium-high heat and then cook the chicken pieces until golden brown on both sides. Remove the chicken pieces and reserve them on a plate. Add the cardamom pods, cloves and cinnamon stick to the hot butter, and stir in the remaining spice mix. Add half of the cooked rice and gently stir to combine it with the fragrant butter. Fold in the remaining rice and layer the chicken thighs deeply in the rice.

5. Bring the saffron water just to a boil and pour it over the rice. Close the pot tightly and finish cooking in the oven for 30 to 40 minutes.

6. Meanwhile, in a small non-reactive pan, combine the ingredients for the condiment and bring them to a boil over high heat. Lower the heat and simmer until reduced by half. Pour the sauce into a non-reactive serving bowl.

7. Serve the chicken rice garnished with the crisply fried shallot onions and accompanied by the chili-vinegar sauce condiment.

8. Garnish with crisply fried shallot onions

THAI STEAMED CHICKEN CURRY

Usually purchased from a hawker, this curry is like a savory custard steamed in small banana leaf bowls. Along with some rice, it makes a good quick lunch or dinner. Steamed curry also makes a great do-ahead dish when you're planning a special dinner. There are many varieties of steamed curry available on the streets and in the markets of Thailand. Feel free to substitute minced fish, seafood, textured soy protein or even diced tofu for the chicken.

right: Damnoen Saduak floating market in Thailand

SPICE PASTE

1 stalk lemon grass,
  trimmed and finely minced
1 tbsp/15 mL galanga, minced
3 green chilies
1 tsp/5 mL peppercorns
3 shallot onions, minced
3 cloves garlic, minced
½ inch/1 cm fresh turmeric
1 tsp/5 mL shrimp paste

MAIN INGREDIENTS

¾ to 1 lb/325 to 500 g minced lean chicken
¾ cup/175 mL thick, coconut milk
1 egg plus 1 egg yolk
2 tbsp/30 mL fish sauce
Banana leaves, fresh or frozen

METHOD

1. Using a mortar and pestle or a small blender or food processor, pound or grind the spice paste ingredients in the order given until they form a coarse paste. Prepare your steamer, making sure you have plenty of boiling water. Choose a sturdy, heat-proof platter that will fit in your steamer and will hold the bowls of steamed curry safely. Prepare all remaining ingredients and have at hand.

2. Combine the minced chicken with 2 tbsp/30 mL of the spice paste, mixing very well. (Any remaining spice paste can be wrapped and frozen for future use.)

3. Stir in the coconut milk, egg, egg yolk and fish sauce and mix very well.

4. Line 4 to 6 small heat-proof bowls with banana leaf and divide the curry mixture equally among them. (Alternatively, using 6-inch/15-cm diameter circles of banana leaf, 2 at a time, and toothpicks, fashion small bowls and fill these with the curry mixture.)

5. Steam the chicken curry for 15 to 20 minutes. To avoid getting scalded, carefully remove the chicken curry from the steamer and serve.

THAI CURRY BRAISED FISH

Choo Chi Pla is the Thai name for this fine example of Thai Palace cuisine. The sauce is not overly spicy, nor is there a lot of it — reflecting the restraint and subtlety of the chefs of Thai royalty. The street version of this dish, known as *Pla Pad Pet* (literally, spicy fried fish) is not refined or very subtle at all. The sauce is very hot, and there is quite a bit more of it to accompany the larger amount of rice that would make up a commoner's meal.

SEASONING

2 to 3 kaffir lime leaves
1 to 2 tbsp/15 to 30 mL Thai curry paste

MAIN INGREDIENTS

Cream from 2 cans (14-oz/400 mL size)
   coconut milk
2 to 3 tsp/10 - 15 mL fish sauce, or to taste
Sugar and salt to taste
3 fish steaks about ½ lb/250 g each

GARNISH

Green onion sliced on a sharp angle,
   fresh coriander leaves and thinly sliced
   red chilies

METHOD

1. Prepare all ingredients and have at hand. Preheat a nonstick frying pan over medium-high heat.

2. Add 2 to 4 tbsp/30 to 60 mL of the coconut cream to the frying pan and reduce it by boiling vigorously while stirring, until the cream separates. Do not allow the cream to burn.

3. Add the kaffir lime leaves and the curry paste and stir well, allowing the coconut oil to absorb the aromatic oils from the curry paste and kaffir lime leaves.

4. Add half the remaining coconut cream, a dash of fish sauce, a pinch of sugar and salt and bring to a boil.

5. Carefully add the fish steaks to the boiling sauce. Add more coconut cream until the boiling sauce reaches at least half-way up the sides of the steaks. Cook the fish for 3 to 4 minutes, and then carefully turn the steaks over and continue cooking. It is important to control the heat so that the sauce does not burn.

6. Reduce the sauce until very thick and coating the fish. Taste and adjust seasoning adding more sugar or fish sauce as desired.

7. Garnish and serve.

THAI GRILLED FISH

he amount of dill used in northern Thai dishes comes as a surprise to many Westerners. It's always an unexpected delight to find familiar flavors in exotic situations. I liked to use this wonderful marinade with fresh halibut cheeks when I was catering for film crews in Vancouver.

SPICE PASTE

1 tbsp/15 mL coarsely chopped lemon grass
1 tbsp/15 mL coarsely chopped coriander root
2 tsp/10 mL coarsely chopped galanga
2 to 4 red chilies, coarsely chopped
2 tbsp/30 mL coarsely chopped dill stems

SEASONING

1 tbsp/15 mL palm sugar or brown sugar
2 tbsp/30 mL fish sauce
Coarse salt to taste
Fresh juice of 1 lime
3 tbsp/45 mL oil

MAIN INGREDIENTS

4 fish steaks, about ½ lb/250 g each

above: Koh Panyee, Thailand

METHOD

1. Prepare all ingredients and have at hand. Using a mortar and pestle or a small blender or food processor, pound or grind the spice paste ingredients in the order given until they form a coarse paste. Combine the spice paste with the seasoning ingredients and mix well.

2. Marinate the fish in the spice-paste-seasoning mixture in a non-reactive dish for 2 to 4 hours.

3. Preheat a grill or barbecue. Grill the fish over a medium-hot fire until done (6 to 8 minutes per side) about 10 to 15 minutes.

THAI FISH AND EGGPLANT CURRY

The real art (and much of the time) behind Thai curry making lies in the preparation of the curry paste; once you have the paste, the rest is quick and easy. Sadly, busy Thai home cooks no longer have the time to spend carefully pounding a perfect curry paste. Prepared curry pastes, whether from a wet market vendor or a supermarket, have become a convenience food in most Thai kitchens these days. This recipe is just as tasty made with any quick-cooking vegetable in place of the eggplant.

SEASONING

- 1 to 3 tbsp/15 to 45 mL Thai green curry paste
- 3 fresh lime leaves
- 2 to 4 fresh red chilies, cut in half lengthwise (optional)

MAIN INGREDIENTS

- 1 14-oz/400 mL can coconut milk, separated
- 1 to 1 ¼ lb/500 to 625 g firm-fleshed white fish, cut into large pieces
- 1 cup/250 mL Thai eggplants, cut into 4 pieces each
- 1 to 2 tbsp/15 to 30 mL fish sauce, or to taste
- Sugar and salt to taste
- Leaves from 2 or more sprigs of Thai basil

GARNISH

- A dollop of thick coconut cream, flowers and sprigs of Thai basil and diagonal slices of fresh red chilies

METHOD

1. Prepare all ingredients and have at hand.

2. Heat a non-reactive, heavy-bottomed, deep pan over medium heat. Add 3 generous spoonfuls of the coconut cream and cook, stirring until reduced and the coconut oil begins to separate. The cream may brown, but do not let it burn.

3. Add the lime leaves and chilies and cook for ½ minute. Add the curry paste. Cook until fragrant and well mixed, about 1 minute.

4. Add the fish pieces and stir gently to coat them with the frying paste. Continue to cook to allow the flavors to penetrate the fish. Do not allow the paste to scorch.

5. Add the thin coconut milk, the remaining coconut cream (reserving a dollop for garnish), the fish sauce and a pinch of sugar and salt. Stir gently and bring to a boil. Add the eggplant, then reduce the heat to a simmer. Cook for 5 minutes.

6. Taste the sauce and adjust the seasoning adding sugar, fish sauce, chilies or salt as desired. Stir in the basil leaves. Garnish and serve.

THAI EGGPLANTS

Thai eggplants are quite small, and when quartered they are perfect for this recipe. If you substitute the larger type of eggplant, chop into bite-size pieces to measure 1 cup/250 mL.

STEAMED FISH WITH CHILI AND LIME

The first time I had this dish it was mid-winter in Montreal, Quebec. I had been invited to join Khun Tong and Madame Song for a staff dinner after closing at their Thai restaurant. Everyone sat around a big table loaded with the home-style dishes that Tong and Song cooked best. A deck of cards and a bottle of whisky was sent around and we passed the winter evening as if we were back in some village in Laos or Thailand. The sauce was so delicious and so hot, I was sure I'd never be able to reproduce it – but here it is!

SEASONING

5 slices of galanga
1 stalk lemon grass, trimmed, bruised and
    cut into 3-inch/8-cm pieces
2 to 3 kaffir lime leaves
½ cup/125 mL coarsely chopped garlic
2 tbsp/30 mL Thai roasted chili flakes
⅓ cup/75 mL fish sauce
½ cup/125 mL lime juice

MAIN INGREDIENTS

1 medium-sized fish (1 to 2 lbs/500 g
    to 1 kg), cleaned, scaled and dried

GARNISH

Your choice of fresh herbs

METHOD

1. Prepare your steamer, making sure you have plenty of boiling water. Choose a deep, heat-proof serving platter that will fit in your steamer and will hold the fish with room to spare. Prepare all ingredients and have at hand.

2. Place the fish on the heat-proof platter. Stuff the fish with the galanga, lemon grass and kaffir lime leaves. Place the platter in the steamer, being careful not to get scalded.

3. Steam the fish over boiling water for approximately 15 to 20 minutes.

4. Meanwhile, in a small non-reactive bowl combine the garlic, chili flakes, fish sauce and lime juice.

5. Once the fish is cooked, carefully remove the platter from the steamer. Pour the chili and lime juice mixture over and around the fish. Garnish and serve.

PRAWN SATAY

raditional satay is a Muslim dish, linked to the cuisines of Indonesia and Malaysia. Its popularity, however, has taken it all over the world, resulting in many regional variations. This Thai version is very simple with a light flavor emphasizing the fresh seafood. Feel free to substitute scallops for the prawns or even use the marinade on a whole fish prior to grilling.

SEASONING

1 clove garlic, minced
1 coriander root, minced
1 tsp/5 mL turmeric powder or
   a small piece of fresh turmeric root
1 tsp/5 mL sugar
Salt to taste
1 tbsp/15 mL vegetable oil

MAIN INGREDIENTS

15 to 20 large prawns,
   peeled with tails left on

GARNISH

Fresh lettuce leaves, slices of cucumber,
   tomato wedges, sprigs of fresh parsley
   and wedges of shallot onion

METHOD

1. Soak 15 to 20 small wooden skewers in a glass of water for 1 hour minimum.

2. In a mortar and pestle or small blender or food processor, pound or grind the garlic and coriander root together. Add the remaining seasoning ingredients and mix well.

3. Mix the prawns with the seasoning mixture and marinate for at least 30 to 40 minutes. Meanwhile, preheat a grill or barbecue.

4. Thread the prawns lengthwise on the skewers. Grill or barbecue 5 to 7 minutes until done.

5. Serve immediately on a garnished plate, accompanied by Thai cucumber relish (see page 105) or your favorite hot sauce.

left: Buddhas at Wat Mahathat, Bangkok

GARLIC AND BASIL STIR-FRIED MUSSELS

his recipe, easy to prepare and quick to make, is a great side dish to fill out a menu, or wonderful on its own accompanied by a bowl of plain rice or some crusty French bread and a cold glass of beer. You can substitute a fresh lobster for the mussels. Just section the lobster or have the fish monger do it.

SPICE PASTE

3 small fresh red or green chilies,
   coarsely chopped
2 cloves garlic, chopped
6 to 8 fresh coriander roots, coarsely chopped

SEASONING

1 tbsp/15 mL fish sauce
1 to 2 tbsp/15 to 30 mL oyster sauce

MAIN INGREDIENTS

2 to 3 tbsp/30 to 45 mL vegetable oil
½ cup/125 mL chicken stock, water or beer
1 lb/500 g fresh mussels, trimmed and cleaned.
3 sprigs of fresh basil, Thai or other, coarsely
   chopped

GARNISH

Sprigs of fresh basil and sliced red chilies

above: Traditional Thai greeting, "Wai"

METHOD

1. Using a mortar and pestle or a small blender or food processor, pound or grind the spice paste ingredients until they form a coarse paste. Prepare all the remaining ingredients and have at hand.

2. Preheat a wok or other deep, heavy-bottomed pan over high heat and then add the oil. As soon as the oil is hot, add the spice paste and stir well to combine. Cook for about ½ minute while while the spice paste imparts its flavor to the oil.

3. Add the fish sauce, oyster sauce and chicken stock. Stir until the mixture comes to a boil.

4. Add the mussels and stir, coating them with the sauce until the sauce returns to a boil. Cover the pan and cook until the mussels open (about 6-8 minutes). Taste the sauce and adjust the seasoning, adding sugar, fish sauce or oyster sauce as desired.

5. Discard any mussels that do not open and stir in the coarsely chopped basil.

6. Garnish and serve immediately.

FISH SAUCE WITH CHILIES

At a Thai hawker's stall, you are likely to notice a set of four covered dishes. One contains sliced serrano chilies in vinegar (to adjust the sourness of a dish), another holds roasted chili flakes (for heat), the third has sugar (to counter the heat) and the final one usually contains a fiery all-purpose mix of fish sauce, lime juice and chilies. The Thai believe that you should have a lot of options when it comes to the final flavor of a dish. This condiment is great for adjusting salty and hot flavors either at the table or during cooking. The number of chilies you use is up to you: add a few pieces for color or several for an intensely hot sauce. The sauce stores well for up to one week in the refrigerator.

MAIN INGREDIENTS

1 clove garlic
¼ cup/60 mL fish sauce
red and green chilies, to taste
3 to 4 tbsp/45 to 60 mL fresh lime juice
Salt and sugar to taste

METHOD

1. In a mortar and pestle or with the side of a knife, crush the garlic to a rough paste. Transfer the paste to a small bowl.

2. Slice the chilies on the diagonal and add them to the garlic in the bowl.

3. Stir in the fish sauce and lime juice. Taste and adjust seasoning, adding salt, sugar or more fresh lime juice as desired.

SOUR FISH SAUCE

This condiment is great for adjusting salty and sour flavors either at the table or during cooking. Consider it a versatile all-purpose seasoning or condiment. This sauce is best when prepared at the last minute.

MAIN INGREDIENTS

¼ cup/60 mL fish sauce
3 tbsp/45 mL fresh lime juice
Sugar to taste

METHOD

1. Combine fish sauce and lime juice in a small serving bowl. (Taste and adjust adding a pinch of sugar or more fresh lime juice as desired.)

CUCUMBER RELISH

A traditional accompaniment to satay, this relish is known as Ajad in Malaysia and Indonesia. But do not limit its use to just satay; it's a great condiment for noodle dishes or with rice or to help tone down a spicy dish at the table.

MAIN INGREDIENTS

1 shallot onion, diced
1 small carrot, peeled and diced
½ English cucumber, seeded and diced
2 to 3 chilies finely sliced (optional)
½ cup/125 mL white vinegar
¾ cup/175 mL white sugar
Salt, pinch

METHOD

1. Prepare all ingredients and have at hand. In a small non-reactive bowl, mix the shallot onion, carrot, cucumber and chilies. Set aside.

2. In a small, non-reactive pan, combine vinegar, sugar and salt and bring to a boil over high heat.

3. Pour the boiling vinegar mixture over the vegetables. (They should be completely immersed.) Let cool to room temperature before using. (Any leftover can be stored in the refrigerator for up to 3 days.)

4. Serve as a relish for grilled or fried foods.

THAI PEANUT SAUCE

The peanut sauce that accompanies traditional satay has as many different variations as there are satay vendors. This version typifies the Thai taste while taking advantage of store-bought crunchy peanut butter. It's quite a simple sauce to make and it keeps exceptionally well — a great accompaniment for cold roast beef or chicken. If you find it is too thick after refrigeration, simply dilute it with some water or coconut milk and reheat it.

SPICE PASTE

1 tbsp/15 mL lemon grass, minced
2 to 3 coriander roots, minced
2 cloves garlic, minced
1 shallot onion, minced
1 tsp/5 mL chili flakes
½ tsp/2 mL ground cumin seed
½ tsp/2 mL ground coriander seed
½ tsp/2 mL shrimp paste

SEASONING

1 to 2 tbsp/15 to 30 mL tamarind water
1 to 2 tbsp/15 to 30 mL sugar
Salt to taste
Fresh lime juice to taste

MAIN INGREDIENTS

2 tbsp/30 mL vegetable oil
1 cup/250 mL coconut milk
3 to 4 tbsp/45 to 60 mL unsweetened crunchy-style peanut butter

METHOD

1. Prepare all ingredients and have at hand. Using a mortar and pestle or small blender or food processor, pound or grind the spice paste ingredients in the order given until they form a coarse paste.

2. Heat a small saucepan on medium heat and add the oil. When the oil is hot, gently fry the spice paste until it smells fragrant and begins to change color. Add the coconut milk, tamarind water and sugar. Stir the mixture and bring to a low boil.

3. Add the peanut butter and stir carefully until it is thoroughly mixed with the sauce. Taste and adjust seasoning, adding salt, sugar, a dash of fish sauce or fresh lime juice to taste.

CHAPTER 4

Hong Kong

The prime gateway to the rest of China, Hong Kong is a curious anomaly. It is an energetic paragon of the virtues of capitalism in what is officially the largest Communist country in the world. Once a British colony, Hong Kong was handed back to China on July 1, 1997. To the casual observer nothing has changed. A new flag, the presence of the Chinese army scattered amongst city's populace perhaps; but the warmth and vitality of this city still leaves one awestruck.

Cantonese cuisine is undoubtedly one of the great cuisines of the world. The fact that it has had such a strong influence on so many other Asian and Southeast Asian cultures is testament to its continuing popularity. Because of this, we decided to do some research in Hong Kong, home to many of the most brilliant Cantonese chefs. Perhaps what makes Cantonese cuisine so popular is the fact that it is – like the city itself – still evolving, resisting the urgings of classicists to define it once and for all. Even a short stay in this city will make you realize Hong Kong is a hotbed of competition when it comes to good restaurants.

When talking about Cantonese cuisine the discussion often turns to some of the very exotic ingredients that can be seen on expensive menus. The beliefs that have shaped this exotic aspect of Cantonese cuisine are, for the most part, ancient ones. One of the primary beliefs that has guided the majority of Chinese regional cuisines is based upon the principles of traditional medicine, in other words: Eat it, it's good for you!

China is a very old culture, and the Chinese have endured many hard lessons from which we can benefit. Their early agricultural practices were often unreliable. Thus, hardship and famine had an important impact on the diet. From these hard times came the belief that, as the saying goes, "Anything that walks with its back to the sun, is fit to eat." This belief inspired cooks in times of famine as well as bounty as they discovered new ways of working with new ingredients.

Another aspect that many people overlook when they consider Asian culinary tradition is the fact that, for ordinary Asians, food is a primary source of family and community entertainment.

In the old days before modern entertainment media, families gathered for meals around the dinner table. These traditions continue to this day, but with a twist: My good friend Johnny Chin has family all over Hong Kong. The high cost and incredibly small size of two- and three-room Hong Kong apartments has kept Johnny's immediate family spread out all over the city. The only place big enough for his family members to sit together for a meal is at a restaurant table. The story is the same for millions of Hong Kong residents. Most Hong Kong apartments have tiny kitchens. With such limited space to cook in, only the oldest and the youngest members of the family eat at home. The rest of the family eat out – breakfast, lunch and dinner

It is said that, with six and a half million inhabitants and several thousand restaurants, Hong Kong has the highest per capita number of eating places anywhere in the world. I can't think of a better reason to visit!

HONG KONG NOODLE SOUP

When I go to Hong Kong I like to visit Mm Hung To, executive chef of the Mouth Kitchen Restaurant in Kowloon. After a busy day, he likes to get out and share a huge bowl of noodle soup with some friends. This recipe is a straightforward version, but feel free to elaborate by adding duck or chicken from the Chinese barbecue or other kinds of quick-cooking seafood, such as scallops or squid.

SEASONING

1 tbsp/15 mL light soy sauce
2 to 3 tsp/10 to 15 mL salt
2 tsp/10 mL sugar
Sesame oil, a few drops to taste
¼ tsp/1 mL white pepper, or to taste
2 tbsp/30 mL Chinese wine, or whiskey

MAIN INGREDIENTS

8 cups/2 L boiling water
¾ to 1 lb/375 to 500 g fresh egg noodles
5 to 6 cups/1.25 to 1.5 L chicken stock
15 large prawns, peeled
½ lb/250 g Chinese barbecue pork, sliced
   (or any cold, leftover cooked meat)
2 green onions, cut in 1-inch/2.5-cm
   sections
2 small Shanghai bok choy, quartered
   lengthwise, trimmed and cleaned
   or any tender quick cooking vegetable
   such as water cress

GARNISH

White pepper and sprigs of fresh
   coriander

METHOD

1. Prepare all ingredients and have at hand. In a deep pan bring the stock to a boil. Adjust the heat to a slow simmer and season the stock with the salt, sugar, sesame oil, white pepper and Chinese wine. Add the pork and the green onion.

2. In a large pan, cook the egg noodles with the boiling water until just done (3 to 4 minutes from time the water returns to a boil). Quickly rinse noodles with cold running water, then drain well and place them in a deep tureen or large soup bowl. Toss with the light soy sauce.

3. While the noodles are cooking, add the Shanghai bok choy and prawns to the simmering stock, and cook to your liking. Remove from the stock and arrange them on top of the noodles.

4. Now remove the pork from the stock and arrange on top of noodles and bok choy.

5. Increase the heat under the stock, taste and adjust the seasoning, adding salt or sugar as desired.

6. Carefully pour the hot soup over the noodles to cover them and serve garnished with fresh coriander leaves and a sprinkle of white pepper.

CANTONESE CLAY POT RICE

The clay pot rice is a dish with a long history. It is uncommon to find it in modern Asian restaurants, but it shows up on the streets and in the smaller out-of-the-way restaurants in Asia and even North America. The first time I was served this dish I sent it back to the kitchen because the bottom was slightly burned and there was a faint odor of burned rice. The chef came out with a furious look on his face and insisted I accept the dish. Years later I learned that a very controlled scorching of the bottom of the pot is considered a hallmark of this dish. This burning is, of course, optional. If you want to modernize this recipe, you can combine all the ingredients in an electric rice cooker and cook according to the manufacturer's instructions.

SEASONING

1 tbsp/15 mL ginger, minced
2 tsp/10 mL Chinese wine, or whiskey
2 tsp/10 mL oyster sauce
1 tsp/5 mL sesame oil
2 tsp/10 mL cornstarch
2 green onions, white part only,
   sliced finely
White pepper, pinch

é

MAIN INGREDIENTS

3 boneless chicken thighs
   cut into 3 pieces each
4 cups/1 L long grain white rice
4 dried Chinese black mushrooms
8 dried lily flowers
2 cups/500 mL chicken stock
   (or 2 cups/500 mL liquid from the
   soaking mushrooms and lily flowers)
1 cup/250 mL water

METHOD

1. Soak the rice in water (enough to cover) for 4 hours or overnight.

2. Combine the seasoning ingredients. Marinate the chicken pieces in the seasoning for at least 1 hour. Meanwhile, prepare all the remaining ingredients and have at hand.

3. Soak the Chinese mushrooms in 2 cups/500 mL very hot water for 15 to 20 minutes. Drain well. Trim off the stems and discard. Cut the caps in half.

4. Soak lily flowers in 1 cup/250 mL very hot water for 15 minutes. Drain.

5. Drain the rice and place it in a heavy-bottomed pan. Add the stock and the water and then the mushrooms, lily flowers and chicken pieces.

6. Cover and bring to a boil over high heat. Lower the heat to medium-low and continue to cook the rice without opening the lid for 20 minutes or until done. (You can open the lid to check on the rice after the 20 minutes.)

CANTONESE FRIED RICE

This dish is popular on most Chinese restaurant menus, where you'll likely find it named Yang Chow Fried Rice. Feel free to substitute any of the ingredients if you find prawns unavailable or have some leftovers to use up. Work with what's in your budget and your fridge.

SEASONING

1 tbsp/15 mL Chinese wine, or whiskey
2 tsp/10 mL cornstarch
¼ cup/60 mL chicken stock, heated

ė

MAIN INGREDIENTS

3 tbsp/45 mL oil
15 large shrimp, peeled and halved
    lengthwise
1 cup/250 mL slivered barbecued pork,
    or any cold leftover cooked meat
½ cup/125 mL finely shredded
    white or green onion,
3 cups/750 mL leftover cooked rice
    (see sidebar)
2 large eggs, beaten
1 tsp/5 mL salt
Salt, sugar and white pepper to taste

GARNISH

Coarsely chopped fresh coriander and
    green onions.

METHOD

1. Prepare all ingredients and have at hand. Marinate the shrimp with the cornstarch and wine for 15 minutes.

2. Heat a wok or large frying pan over high heat and add the oil.

3. As soon as the oil begins to form a haze, add the marinated shrimp and stir-fry briefly until they change color. Add the barbecued pork and continue to stir-fry until heated through. Add the green onion and salt and stir-fry until fragrant (1 to 2 minutes maximum).

4. Add the rice. Stir-fry until the rice is well mixed with the shrimp, pork and green onion.

5. Add the stock, a little at a time gently stirring until all the stock has been absorbed. Add the beaten egg in the same manner, and continue to cook the mixture until the rice grains separate and the egg is cooked.

6. Taste and adjust the seasoning adding salt, sugar or white pepper as desired. Garnish and serve.

LEFTOVER RICE

Leftover rice is ideal for this recipe because it is drier. If you don't have any leftover rice on hand, you can use fresh-cooked rice — but use slightly less water when cooking for a drier result.

above: *Shopping in Hong Kong — so much to choose!*

STUFFED SWEET PEPPERS

My very first job in charge of a kitchen was at a private school where the students came from Hong Kong, Malaysia and other parts of Southeast Asia. Once a week a group of students would come into the kitchen and cook a dish from home that they missed. That was how I first learned to make stuffed peppers. Over the years, I've modified my recipe giving it more of a pan-Asian flavor, reflecting the tastes of Hong Kong, Korea, and Malaysia.

SEASONING

2 tbsp/30 mL sesame oil
2 tbsp/30 mL soy sauce
1 tbsp/15 mL dry red chilies, ground
2 tsp/10 mL black pepper, coarsely ground
4 cloves garlic, minced
2 green onions, minced
1 inch/2 cm cube of fresh gingerroot, minced

MAIN INGREDIENTS

1 lb/500 g lean ground pork, chicken, turkey or beef
2 tbsp/30 mL roasted sesame seeds
1 large egg
4 to 5 sweet bell peppers (the more colorful the better) stem on, cut in half length-wise with seeds and veins removed

GARNISH

Sprigs of fresh coriander and roasted sesame seeds

METHOD

1. Combine all seasoning and main ingredients except for the sweet peppers and oil. Mix well. (This mixture can be refrigerated for several days or frozen for later use.)

2. Fill the pepper halves with the meat mixture and smooth the surface of the filling.

3. Heat a frying pan on medium heat and add the oil. Fry the stuffed peppers, meat side down, for 25 to 30 minutes until they are deep reddish-brown on the bottom and cooked through. Alternatively, after the meat has browned, finish cooking them in a preheated 350° F/180° C oven for 20 minutes or until done.

4. Garnish and serve.

PERUVIAN CHINESE BARBECUED CHICKEN

Years ago while traveling to Japan and Thailand, I took a layover in New York City to visit my friend Melanie Reffes. She made sure that I visited a Peruvian-Chinese restaurant called the Flor de Mayo, on Broadway. The result of that visit is this succulent chicken created by the fusion of two very different cultures colliding in a family kitchen. They call it Pollo a la Brasa, a whole marinated chicken grilled on a spit. If you cannot find Chinese black vinegar, substitute balsamic vinegar.

SEASONING

3 tbsp/45 mL honey
3 tbsp/45 mL peanut oil
6 tbsp/90 mL black vinegar
3 tbsp/45 mL dark soy sauce
1 tbsp/15 mL chili paste,
    or 4 red chilies pounded to a paste
1 tsp/5 mL sesame oil
4 tbsp/60 mL cumin powder
2 tsp/10 mL coriander powder
½ tsp/2 mL garam masala
1 tbsp/15 mL salt

MAIN INGREDIENTS

1 Medium chicken split down the back,
    or 1 to 2 lbs/500 g to 1 kg
    chicken thighs

METHOD

1. Prepare all ingredients and have at hand. Combine the seasoning ingredients and mix well.

2. Open the chicken so that it lays flat. Trim away any loose skin or fat and cut off the wing tips. Marinate the chicken in the seasoning in a non-reactive dish for 2 hours or overnight.

3. Preheat a grill or barbeque. Grill the chicken over a medium fire until done (35 to 40 minutes) or roast the chicken in an 375° F/190° C oven until done, about 1 hour. Allow the chicken to rest on a platter for 10 minutes before serving.

*left: A selection of Hong Kong barbecued
meats — a popular late night meal*

BOURBON CHICKEN IN A WOK

In many cultures special events are celebrated at the table by sharing a beautifully cooked and presented whole turkey, duck, goose or suckling pig fresh from the oven. However, home ovens were either impractical or unpopular in many Asian cultures. This recipe is a great Asian approach to cooking a whole chicken. The result is a succulent bird with a beautiful mahogany glaze and superb flavor. It is important to have a good stable base for your wok in order to safely turn the chicken during cooking.

CHICKEN SAFETY

To cook evenly, the chicken cannot be too cold. You can safely allow the chicken to sit for no more than 30 minutes before starting this recipe.

right: Traditional production of soy sauce in Hong Kong

SEASONING

4 whole star anise
6 tbsp/90 mL soy sauce
6 tbsp/90 mL sugar
6 tbsp/90 mL rice vinegar
4 tbsp/60 mL bourbon

MAIN INGREDIENTS

6 tbsp/90 mL oil
1 medium-sized chicken, trimmed of excess fat and skin

METHOD

1. Using a large sharp cleaver or heavy knife cut the chicken through the breast bone, but do not cut the chicken in half or through the backbone. Open the carcass so that it lies flat. You may need to nick the backbone in order to lay the chicken flat, skin side down.

2. Place the chicken on a plate and cover it with plastic wrap while you clean up and prepare the remaining ingredients (see sidebar).

3. Preheat a wok over high heat. Add the oil and carefully stir to coat the sides of the wok. When the oil is hot, carefully place the chicken, skin side down, in the wok. Allow the front of the chicken to turn golden brown before carefully turning the chicken one quarter-turn to cook its side. Turn the chicken over to its other side to fry golden brown as well. Carefully remove the chicken from the wok and place it on a platter.

4. Add the seasoning ingredients to the oil in the wok and stir until the sugar has melted and the sauce comes to a boil. Return the chicken to the wok, skin side down. Reduce the heat until the sauce is at a gentle boil. Cover and cook 10 minutes.

5. Carefully turn the chicken one quarter-turn onto its side. Cover the pan and cook 3 to 5 minutes. Repeat this for the other side of the chicken. Test the chicken to see if it is cooked through by piercing the biggest part of the thigh with a skewer. The juices should run almost clear.

6. When the chicken is cooked, turn it skin side up and push it part way up the side of the wok. Increase the heat and baste the chicken with the sauce while the sauce reduces. In a few minutes you will have a thick dark glaze. Turn off the heat.

7. Transfer the chicken to a cutting board, then carefully cut it in half lengthwise. Cut each half into 2-inch/5-cm sections, reassembling the chicken onto a serving platter.

TWICE-COOKED DUCK

n this twice-cooked recipe, duck breasts are marinated, steamed and then shallow-fried. The duck becomes so fragrant and rich that it is best enjoyed in thin slices. This is an ideal appetizer or cocktail snack that can be prepared ahead of time and finished moments before serving. Be sure to leave lots of preparation time for this wonderful dish.

SEASONING

1 tbsp/15 mL star anise, lightly crushed
1 tbsp/15 mL Chinese peppercorns
2 to 3 oz/50 to 85 g fresh gingerroot, peeled, sliced and bruised
5 large green onions, cut in 1 to 2-inch/2.5 to 5 cm pieces
2 ½ tbsp/37 mL salt

MAIN INGREDIENTS

2 to 3 boneless duck breasts, about 1 ¼ lb/600 g total
1 tbsp/15 mL dark soy
1 tbsp/15 mL rice vinegar
Vegetable oil (enough for shallow-frying)

GARNISH

Thin slices of cucumber and green onion

METHOD

1. Clean, trim and dry the duck breasts. Prepare all remaining ingredients and have at hand.

2. In a mortar and pestle, gently pound the seasoning ingredients until the salt is damp. Rub the duck breasts with the seasoning and then wrap them in plastic wrap. Marinate the breasts for 2 to 8 hours in the refrigerator.

3. Unwrap the duck breasts and steam them with the seasoning ingredients for 1 ½ hours. Be sure to suspend the duck pieces on a rack set above a heat-proof bowl or pan in order to collect the drippings. While the duck steams, check the water level in your steamer and add more boiling water if the level gets low.

4. Cool the duck for 10 minutes, then gently brush off any remaining marinade ingredients. Combine the soy sauce and the rice vinegar and brush over each duck breast. Place the duck breasts back on the rack and allow them to air dry in a cool place or refrigerator for 3 hours. (At this point the duck breasts can be covered and refrigerated for up to 2 days.)

5. Heat the oil in a deep pan, suitable for shallow-frying. When the oil is hot, shallow-fry the duck, starting skin side down, until the skin and underside of each piece is dark mahogany in color. Drain the fried duck well on paper towel and allow to cool briefly.

6. Slice each piece thinly while it's still hot. Garnish and serve.

left: Freshly roasted duck at the market, ready to serve

BRAISED PRAWNS

T his dish is another great example of infusing hot oil with aromatics, in this case ginger and green onion. Very quick and easy to make, these prawns are a great side dish or appetizer.

SEASONING

1 ½ tbsp/22 mL Chinese wine, or whiskey
1 ½ tbsp/22 mL rice vinegar
1 tbsp/15 mL water
Salt, pinch
1 inch/2.5 cm of fresh gingerroot,
    sliced ¼ inch/5 mm thick
2 green onions, cut into 2 inch/5 cm
    lengths
⅔ cup/150 mL sugar

MAIN INGREDIENTS

¼ cup/60 mL oil
1 ½ lbs/750 g large prawns,
    trimmed, with shells left on

METHOD

1. Combine the Chinese wine, rice vinegar, water and salt. Set aside. Prepare all remaining ingredients and have at hand.

2. Preheat a wok over medium-high heat and add the oil. When the oil is hot, add the ginger and green onion and stir-fry for 10 seconds. Carefully add the wine mixture along with the sugar. Stir until the sugar is dissolved and the mixture is boiling.

3. Add the prawns and stir to coat well. Continue to cook, boiling vigorously, while stirring occasionally to ensure the prawns cook evenly. Reduce the sauce to a sticky glaze that coats the prawns. Do not allow the sauce to scorch. Serve.

STIR-FRIED PRAWNS WITH SHANGHAI BOK CHOY

Here is a great stir-fry dish with all the wonderful aromas of classic Cantonese cookery. During the taping of *Entrée To Asia*, we visited several chefs who explained the importance of aromatic oil. Several times a week, they would infuse hot oil with aromatic ingredients like shallot onions, green onions, leeks and small amounts of ginger and garlic. This oil would then be used for stir frying, adding subtle complexity to the aroma and flavor of the dish.

SEASONING

1 tbsp/15 mL Chinese wine or whiskey
2 tsp/10 mL cornstarch
4 small slices of fresh gingerroot
2 cloves of garlic, bruised
6 thin slices of carrot
Salt, sugar and white pepper to taste

MAIN INGREDIENTS

10 to 12 medium-large prawns,
    peeled with tails left on
2 to 3 tbsp/30 to 45 mL oil
4 Shanghai or baby bok choy,
    stalks and leaves separated and stalks
    cut in to bite-size pieces
1 tsp/5 mL Chinese wine, or whiskey
¼ cup/60 mL chicken broth or water

METHOD

1. Prepare all ingredients and have at hand. Combine the prawns with the 1 tbsp/15 mL Chinese wine and the cornstarch and allow to marinate for 15 minutes.
2. Preheat a wok or deep heavy, frying pan over medium-high heat and add the oil. As soon as the oil is hot, add the ginger, garlic and carrot and stir-fry for a few minutes to infuse the oil with the aromas of the ginger, garlic and carrots.
3. Add the prawns and gently stir-fry for 3 to 4 minutes or just until they change color. Do not overcook.
4. Add the bok choy stalks and stir-fry for another minute. Sprinkle the Chinese wine and a pinch each (or to taste) of salt, sugar and white pepper over the prawns and bok choy as they cook.
5. Add the chicken broth and the bok choy leaves. Stir once and then cover for 1 ½ minutes. Serve.

Our 'Kitchenary' is a collection of ingredients, substitutions and useful kitchen information to help you on your way. Although it is not intended to be a complete compendium of Asian culinary techniques, I hope it covers the more important cooking methods and ingredients relative to this book.

MARKET MADNESS

Shopping for food in an exotic market is exciting, but it takes practice. You'll want to spend an afternoon rooting about your neighborhood Asian market to familiarize yourself with things. Have a good look-around on a Saturday or Sunday when people are shopping for a big family meal. Whether you are looking for an all-in-one supermarket or trying to choose separate markets for meats, seafood and produce, look for the stores that are doing the most business. There should be chaos and noise and the sound of busy cash registers. Take a look at the selection of goods. Does the food look fresh? Are people buying?

Here is the most important part: Get up the nerve to ask questions of other shoppers. If you look for a few customers around your age, not too unlike yourself, you'll likely find they share similar time constraints and have the same concerns about quality as you. Ask them what they think of the store and the selection. And don't be afraid to talk with the shopkeeper or, in a supermarket, the manager. Most of the good stores I have found have knowledgeable people on staff. They also realize that by word of mouth they could gain a lot of new customers. The best part (and this is from personal experience) is that you will meet people who share the same love of cooking that you do. You will gain confidence and your adventure will be more rewarding than simply shopping for groceries!

THE NINE-MONTH RULE

The number one way to improve the flavor of the food that you cook is to observe the nine-month rule. Go right now into your kitchen cupboards, fridge and freezer and get rid of any seasoning, sauce, spice, condiment, oil or any other ingredient that is more than nine months old. Most canned foods are exempt from this rule (there is always an exception to a rule). You may not be left with very much on your shelves, but what you are left with is not stale, oxidized or past-due and therefore has the best flavor to go with your best efforts. Now, when a recipe calls for something you don't have, go and buy a small amount of the ingredient in question, not the super value bulk pack. By keeping fresh, flavorful ingredients in your kitchen, the flavor of the food you prepare will be surprisingly improved.

An additional tip: I like to keep my fresh spices in small, airtight zipper-style bags in the freezer. You will be amazed at how well they keep their best aroma and flavor, especially if you spend the time and effort to dry roast and grind them yourself.

USEFUL COOKING TECHNIQUES

Blanching
You can blanch vegetables hours ahead to help you save time when you start a recipe. Just bring a pot of water to boil, leaving plenty of room for the vegetables. Add the cut-up vegetables and cook for 1 to 5 minutes, depending on the color and the toughness of the vegetables. (Blanch broccoli only until it becomes bright green; carrots and other fibrous or starchy foods take longer to insure

they are approximately "half cooked.") Remove the vegetables from the boiling water and plunge them into a large bowl or sink of cold water. Drain well.

If I need to blanch several different vegetables for different lengths of time, I prefer to use a wire skimmer or a big slotted spoon to remove ingredients from the boiling water, using the same boiling water to blanch each ingredient separately.

Shallow-Frying

Shallow-frying is usually done in a high-sided frying pan, a wok or a Dutch oven using a couple of inches (about 5 cm) of hot oil to fry whole fish, pieces of marinated meat or for frying fritters and other snack foods. Shallow-frying differs from deep-frying only in the amount of oil that is used and in the fact that the food is rarely fully immersed in the oil. Sometimes shallow-frying can be done in advance, and then the rest of the recipe completed at a later time.

Shallow-frying is done at 350 to 400°F (180 to 200°C). You can use a thermometer to check your heat, or you can dip a wooden chopstick just under the surface of the oil, watching the speed and volume of air bubbles that come from the chopstick. A moderate flow of bubbles indicates near 350°F (180°C), while a very fast flow indicates the upper limit, close to 400°F (200°C). Exact temperature control is not essential.

Steaming

Steaming is a very efficient and healthful way to cook many different types of food. Caution is required, however, as steam is very hot and can burn you quite badly. Whenever I am steaming food, I turn off the heat and open the steamer to allow built-up steam to disperse before adding or removing food to or from the steamer. Always lift the lid of a steamer away from you, as it is the first blast of steam that is the hottest.

My steamer is an all-in-one unit with an ample pot for the boiling water, two stacking steamer levels and an attractive domed lid that fits on top. It was very inexpensive and made of aluminum. (I don't normally recommend cooking with aluminum since it is a reactive metal. However, when steaming the food rarely comes in direct contact with the metal, so you need not worry about the food changing flavor or discoloring.) You can also buy bamboo steamer baskets in most Asian markets. They are designed to sit over a wok. If you don't own a steamer, you can use a roasting pan with a lid or a big enamel Dutch oven as the boiler. To support the dish that the food will be steamed in, use a couple of small heat-proof bowls or some cans that have had both the top and bottom removed. There are also simple metal trivets and racks available that will hold the plate or bowl you are steaming in.

Some electric rice cookers also have steaming options. Use the manufacturer's directions when steaming; you will need to keep a kettle of boiling water handy to make sure the steamer does not run out of boiling water during the cooking process.

Stir-Frying

Stir-frying is a super way to prepare food, but it requires a different way of thinking. Stir-frying requires big heat, and the best source for modern cooks is a gas stove. In a typical Asian kitchen, the wok burner is much hotter than what you may be used to, and when working with that kind of heat you need to stir often to prevent food from burning.

If you don't have a gas stove, don't use a wok, because a wok is designed to work over a live flame. Instead, use a heavy Dutch oven or a big cast-iron frying pan that has the mass to retain the heat you need. Preheat the pan before you add oil so you have enough heat to get the job done.

You also want to limit the size of the dish. If you want to feed more than four, prepare additional dishes instead of increasing the amount of ingredients in a given recipe. This will ensure that your stir-fried dishes will not overwhelm the relatively small amount of heat the typical stove will provide. You need to be well organized in advance: you won't have time for slicing, dicing or measuring while the pan is hot!

Don't rush when stir-frying meats. If you stir too much, the cold pieces of meat will cool the pan, and instead of frying they will begin to simmer in their own juices. Instead, allow the pieces of meat to sear one side at a time. Then stir carefully to turn the pieces over to color on the uncooked side. Once the meat is mostly seared, you can stir more frequently until the pieces are cooked. This is a really good way to compensate for an ordinary stove's lack of heat.

CARE AND FEEDING OF YOUR WOK

If you have a stove that can provide enough heat, a wok is a wonderful tool to work with. There are two traditional types of wok I prefer. One is very common and can be found just about anywhere. It is made of thin steel and has either two small handles, or just one longer wooden handle. I prefer the long handle as it makes it easier to flip the food. The thin metal of these kinds of wok transmit the heat quickly, which is what you want in a good wok.

The other type of wok I like is made of thin cast iron. These are not too heavy, but they are brittle and can break if accidentally dropped. The cast iron wok can hold heat a little better, and this makes it a great choice for the home cook with an underpowered stove. There is a minor drawback with cast-iron woks: they come coated in some kind of metal-oxide to prevent rusting, and it is a really messy job scrubbing them clean before the first use. I use a heavy-duty scrubbing powder and elbow grease to clean this kind of wok before I start to season them. Of course, once this job is done, you will never have to do it again.

Getting your wok ready for use, a process known as "seasoning," is straightforward but can take some time. Some woks come with a varnish or coating that must be removed before you can start this process. Use hot soapy water or paint thinner if the coating on the wok seems to be a varnish. Clean the wok a second time with hot soapy water, to be sure there is no residue remaining from the first cleaning.

Next, with the kitchen fan on high, heat the wok over very high heat; don't worry if it begins to discolor. Take a good bundle of paper towel or scrunch up an old rag and dip it into the cooking oil. Carefully rub a thin coating of oil onto the surface of the wok. This can create quite a bit of smoke, so don't be surprised if the smoke alarm goes off. Remove the wok from the heat and allow it to cool. Repeat this process again and you should be ready to begin your stir-frying adventures. Now you have a nice, seasoned wok it is important not to over-clean it. After stir-frying, and preferably while the wok is still hot, simply clean it out with hot water and a scrubber of your choice. Use soap only if the food was really greasy and then use only a tiny amount of soap to get the job done.

A well-seasoned, well-used wok is nearly black with use. The built-up layers of oil from frequent use create a non-stick, non-reactive coating that makes stir-frying easier and food taste better. Try to avoid simmering very liquid dishes in your wok until you have a really solid seasoning built up. Even then, try to avoid cooking dishes that take time to simmer as this will compromise the protective coating. I won't hesitate, however, to save time by starting a curry, soup or stew in my wok and then transferring it to a suitable pot to finish the cooking.

A final note: Don't leave food in the wok for a long time after it is prepared! I have seen people bring what must have been a wonderful prawn curry to a pot-luck dinner, still in the wok they prepared it in. It looked good on the buffet, but the dish tasted strongly of the metal the wok was make with. The curry reacted with the poorly seasoned wok, and the dish was ruined, along with the seasoning of the wok.

GLOSSARY OF CULINARY TERMS

BAI HORABHA: *See* Thai basil.

BANANA LEAVES: Available frozen in Asian markets. Defrost, wipe with a moist cloth or paper towel and then use as directed in the recipe. You can also use them to decorate platters, trays and buffet tables.

BEAN SPROUTS: Delicate in flavor and very nutritious, bean sprouts are an important food in most Chinese-influenced cuisines. Bean sprouts should be eaten fresh for the best flavor, so use them within a day or two of buying them.

BEET GREENS: The usually discarded leaves and stems of beet root. Rich in vitamins and with a slightly peppery flavor, beet greens make a wonderful stir-fry vegetable.

BOK CHOY: Bright white stems, reminiscent of celery, and deep green leaves typify bok choy. Baby bok choy is often also available and is considered an upscale substitute for the mature variety. Bok choy requires very little cooking time.

BRUISED: Partially crushed, as opposed to slicing or chopping into little pieces. Bruising aromatic ingredients allows them to better impart their flavor to a soup or simmered dish. After the dish is cooked, the bruised ingredient can be easily removed.

CANDLE NUTS: Known as *kemiri* nuts in Malaysia, these oil-rich nuts provide a rich texture to sauces. Candle nuts are always finely ground as part of the *rempah* or spice paste. Do not eat raw candle nuts; you will not feel well afterwards. A good substitute for candle nut is Macadamia nut.

CHILI PEPPERS: Many varieties of chili peppers are finding their way into our markets. Chilies are prized not only for the amount of heat that they can add to a dish but also for their flavor. Generally speaking, the smaller the chili the hotter it will seem, certainly in relation to the amount of chili flavor that it provides. Bigger, fleshier chilies offer more flavor, in relation to heat, and make a good substitute if you want to make a milder dish. The seeds and ribs inside of a chili are the hottest part, so you can remove them if you want to reduce the heat of your recipe while preserving the authentic flavor of the dish. Don't be shy to wear rubber gloves when handling fresh chilies, you might inadvertently touch your eyes or nose after cutting them.

CHILI POWDER/FLAKES: Made from dried chilies, ground or flaked. The Thai like to use roasted chili flakes, which they call *prik pon*. Whole dried red chilies are carefully dry roasted to a lovely brick-red color to improve their flavor before grinding. Substitute ordinary chili flakes or even cayenne powder, but be aware that cayenne can pack a really hot wallop.

CHINESE PEPPERCORNS: Not really a type of peppercorn, but a dried flower that has a distinctly hot and numbing effect on the palate. Popular in Sechuanese cuisine and easy to find in Chinese grocery stores.

CHINESE WINE: Also known as rice wine. This clear or yellowish wine is available in many Asian grocery stores. Used sparingly, Chinese wine imparts an important flavor and aroma to traditional stir-fry dishes and marinades. Many of my friends in Hong Kong like to use scotch whiskey or even bourbon as a substitute.

CINNAMON STICK: Fragrant cinnamon bark rolled into sticks, available in the spice section of most commercial markets or in bulk.

CORIANDER: Also known as cilantro and/or Chinese parsley. One of the most popular and versatile herbs worldwide. The plant provides us with three important ingredients: coriander leaves, roots and seeds.

CORIANDER LEAVES: Used to provide an intense, fresh flavor to soups, stir-fry dishes and salads. Coriander leaves should be added to hot foods at the last moment before serving, to preserve their flavor.

CORIANDER ROOT: Can be used to provide the full coriander taste to long-cooking dishes or marinades without the discoloration or loss of flavor that can happen when cooking with the delicate leaves. The volatile aromatic oils that give fresh coriander its pungent flavor are more concentrated in the root. As the roots are usually trimmed prior to display for sale, you can ask your grocer to save them for you if you have trouble finding the whole plant.

CORIANDER SEEDS: An important ingredient in soups, marinades, curries, pickles and even beer in many different cuisines around the world. The best flavor can be obtained from coriander seeds by dry roasting the whole seeds in a heavy frying pan on medium heat until they release their aroma. The seeds can then be ground or crushed depending on the requirements of the recipe.

CRISPY FRIED GARLIC: A delicious product from Southeast Asia, commercially prepared and used as a garnish for soups, salads and stir-fried noodle dishes. Inexpensive and easy to use.

CUMIN: Similar in shape to caraway seed with a flavor you will recall from store-bought curry powder. Cumin seed is an important spice in many Indian cuisines. Cumin can be used generously to provide strong flavor and aroma, or used in moderation to provide subtle, harmonizing character to a dish. Available in seed form or ground as a powder. The best flavor can be obtained from cumin seed by dry roasting the whole seeds in a heavy frying pan on medium heat until they release their aroma. The seeds can then be ground or crushed depending on the requirements of the recipe.

DARK SOY SAUCE: *See* soy sauce.

EGG NOODLES: Made from egg and wheat flour, these noodles are readily available commercially fresh or dried.

FISH SAUCE: An essential ingredient in the cooking of a number of Southeast Asian cuisines. Thai fish sauce is generally considered superior to fish sauce made in other countries. This clear, amber-brown sauce is made from small, anchovy-like fish that are salted and fermented. You will find that fish sauce has a pungent aroma, but a surprisingly mild flavor. When used as a condiment at the table a small amount of freshly squeezed lime juice is always added to fish sauce to cut the strong aroma. I prefer to use lighter colored premium brands of Thai fish sauce that can be used in a variety of cuisines, both Asian and Western. The next time you make a Caesar salad, or any recipe calling for anchovies, try using a few teaspoons of fish sauce instead!

GAI LAN: Often called Chinese Broccoli, or *pak ka-na* in Thailand, gai lan is similar to broccoli rabe or rapini, but has a mellower flavor. Gai lan can be prepared much the same way as ordinary broccoli, but it should be blanched before stir-frying. Avoid buying gai lan that has blossomed as the flavor can become bitter at this point. A few open yellow flowers are not a problem though.

GALANGA: Associated with the cuisine of Thailand, but used throughout Southeast Asia, *galanga* has a wonderful aroma and flavor that is hard to describe, but not unlike eucalyptus. Galanga is a root of a plant in the ginger family. An important ingredient in Thai curry-pastes and Malaysian rempahs. When sliced and used in soups, it is usually removed before serving or left uneaten. It can be found fresh or dried in Thai, Lao or Vietnamese markets. Dried galanga is inferior in flavor to the fresh variety but will do in a pinch. Soak slices of dried galanga in hot water for at least 25 minutes, or until soft, before using them in any recipe.

GINGER: Now a staple in many Western kitchens as well as Asian ones. Perhaps the most important advice concerning ginger is to not add too much. Fresh ginger can easily unbalance a dish. More and more we see two kinds of ginger in the markets. The traditional mature ginger should have the thick skin cut away before slicing, grating or cubing as directed (although when I'm feeling lazy I skip this!). Young ginger is starting to be more readily available and is superior in flavor and aroma to the mature variety. When buying, choose smooth skinned, plump pieces of ginger. Fresh peeled ginger can be stored in the refrigerator in an airtight jar, covered with whiskey or Chinese wine; later you can use the wine when stir-frying or steaming chicken or seafood. Dry ground ginger is not a substitute for fresh in any recipe in this cookbook.

KAFFIR LIME LEAVES: Also referred to as perfume-lime, citrus or just lime leaves, these are an important ingredient in Thai and Malay cookery. Lime leaves are usually left whole or simply torn in half lengthwise when added to soups, curries and other dishes. They can then be removed before serving, or at the table. An attractive, and edible, garnish can be made by very carefully shredding lime leaves lengthwise with a sharp knife to create a very fine angel hair garnish for Thai curries. Available fresh or dried, you can find these leaves in Thai, Lao or Vietnamese markets.

KARI LEAVES: A legacy from Sri Lanka, these wonderful leaves are hard to find and impossible to substitute. The dried variety has only a hint of the original flavor, but if that is all that is available, then use it. Used primarily in curries and some typical southern Indian stir-fried dishes. You can find fresh kari leaves in Tamil and South Indian markets.

LEMON GRASS: Fresh lemon grass is available in many Thai, Lao, Vietnamese and now even supermarket produce departments. Lemon grass features in barbecue marinades, salads, curry pastes and in soups from all over Southeast Asia. To release the best flavor and aroma, the stalks need to be bruised or chopped before use. Fresh lemon grass will keep for several weeks in the refrigerator. Dried lemon grass can be used by placing several pieces in a bowl and covering with hot water. Let stand for about 20 minutes, then drain.

LIGHT SOY SAUCE: *See* soy sauce.

LILY BUDS, LILY FLOWERS: Often referred to as Golden Needles in Chinese cookbooks, lily buds are an important ingredient in many Chinese-influenced cuisines. Lily buds are the edible dried flower buds of day lilies. Soften them in hot water for 15-20 minutes. Remove the hard knob of the stem prior to cooking.

LIME LEAVES: *See* kaffir lime leaves.

MORTAR AND PESTLE: There is no turning back! Once you start to use a mortar and pestle for grinding fresh spices and aromatics, you will quickly become addicted to the improved flavor of the food you cook. Most mortars and pestles are made of stone, however Thais often use clay mortars with wooden pestles to work specifically with small amounts of moist curry pastes and for bruising lemon grass, garlic and coriander root. Choose a good-sized mortar and pestle over small ones, you will definitely need the room to work in.

As an alternative to a mortar and pestle, there are quite a few styles of small food-processors / grinders available in kitchen shops. They do a very good job of grinding most spice pastes featured in this book. Be sure to follow manufacturer's instructions. Process ingredients in small batches for best results.

MUNG BEAN NOODLE: Featured in salads, stir-fry dishes, hot-pots and soups. Also known as glass noodles or Chinese bean threads, these are very fine transparent noodles made from mung bean flour. Soak in hot, not boiling, water for about 10 minutes before using.

MUSTARD GREENS: Leaves of the mustard plant grown commonly in India and China for their seeds. Mustard greens are available year-round in Asian markets. The giant curled variety has soft satiny leaves and white or yellow blossoms. When rolled between the fingers the leaves give off a sweet, mustardy aroma. A great addition to stir-fry dishes.

NON-REACTIVE: A very important quality for cookware that you use for long-cooking and simmered dishes is that it be non-reactive. Cookware that is stainless steel, ceramic, glass, enamel or, in some cases, anodized all qualify as non-reactive. What's important is that food cannot react chemically with the material the cookware is made of, preventing tinny, metallic or other undesirable flavors from contaminating your good cooking.

OIL: When I stir-fry I prefer to use peanut oil. Not just any peanut oil; I prefer peanut oil from Hong Kong or Kowloon. These oils are not as refined as most North American peanut oils and as a result they have a faint, almost imperceptible, peanut flavor that adds delicious complexity to the food you cook. If you are looking for another suitable oil for stir-frying, then use canola oil. It is ideal for the job. Olive, corn, sunflower and blended oils containing any of these are not suitable for stir-frying; they will burn and contribute an acrid flavor to the dish.

OYSTER SAUCE: A dark brown, ketchup-like sauce with a rich flavor. Ideally made from the extract of oysters, salt, starch and other choice ingredients, there exist many brands of oyster sauce that contain no oyster at all! Read the label carefully to be sure of what you are buying. Oyster sauce is featured in marinades, hot-pots and stir-fry dishes.

PALM SUGAR: Also known as *Gula Melaka* or *Gula Jawa*. A rich, flavorful sugar made from the sweet liquid found in the flower of several varieties of palm tree. Ranging in color from light amber to dark brown, this sugar is an important foil for the heat of many spicy Southeast Asian dishes. I prefer the dark brown Gula Jawa palm sugar from Indonesia. I just use a sharp knife and slice off roughly the amount I need for the recipe in question. Brown sugar, although sweeter, can be substituted for palm sugar in a pinch, but the flavor will not be quite the same.

PANDAN LEAVES: Known in Thailand as *bai toey* and in Malaysia as *daun pandan*, these are the long, narrow leaves of the screw-pine. Used primarily when cooking rice and also to add a unique aroma to desserts and some deep-fried dishes. They have an unmistakable flavor and aroma that is impossible to substitute for. If you can't find them fresh, then look for pandan extract, popular with many Thai and Malay cooks.

RICE: While many varieties of rice exist, for me there is only one variety of choice: Thai Jasmine rice. Fragrant, perfumed, exquisite; these are all appropriate descriptions of jasmine rice. You will find that jasmine rice is easier to cook than basmati rice and it is significantly cheaper to boot. When it comes to cooking rice I use a rice cooker. Rice cookers are indispensable and as common in Asia as toasters are in North America. Rice cookers are affordable, practical and time saving. They can be used to cook long-grain, short-grain, brown and par-boiled rice. For the average family you will need a five or 10 cup model. Choose a rice cooker with a Teflon lining; the other styles are more hassle than they are worth. The model I have has a timer that allows me to set the cooker in the morning and then come home to freshly cooked rice in the evening!

RICE VINEGAR: Made from rice, this colorless vinegar is less acidic than regular white vinegar.

SHALLOT ONIONS: Brown or red in color, shallot onions offer superior flavor and are an authentic ingredient in many Southeast Asian cuisines. They are not to be confused with scallions or green onions. Substitute sweet onions for shallots.

SHRIMP PASTE: A powerful flavoring, dark brown in color, made from salted, dried shrimp. While many varieties exist in the wet-markets of Thailand and Malaysia, each one destined for a different application, here in the West we are limited to one or two choices. Don't let that worry you; just use what is available in your local Asian market. The Thai variety is different from the Malay, but in a pinch you can substitute one for the other, or use anchovy paste.

SOY SAUCE: Made from fermented soy beans, soy sauce is available light, dark or sweet. The light variety is generally used with white meat dishes, more for flavor than color, and the dark type with dark meats and more for color than flavor. Sweet soy, often known as *ketjap manis*, is a typical Indonesian/Malay seasoning made with palm sugar and spices. It makes a versatile seasoning for many dishes.

STAR ANISE: Featured in Chinese and Malay simmered dishes and marinades. The dried form of the star-shaped fruit of an evergreen tree. Use sparingly as it has an intense anise or licorice flavor. Available in the spice section of your market.

STOCK: Everyone will tell you that homemade stock will give you the best flavor, however, let's be realistic about how much time we have to spend in the kitchen. I recommend you substitute canned chicken broth for any recipe calling for stock, whether for soup or for stir-fry dishes. Canned stock often contains salt, so I taste it before I use it for the first time to judge if I need to adjust the seasoning of the dish. Increasingly, I find many excellent canned Asian or Cantonese broths featuring ingredients like dried scallops and Chinese ham. Feel free to use these premium products instead of ordinary canned chicken broth for most of these recipes.

SWEET PEPPER: Bell peppers – red, green, yellow – any one or a variety will do. I like to choose an attractive assortment of colors to brighten up the food I cook.

TAMARIND: The sour-earthy tasting fruit of the Tamarind tree. A popular ingredient in many Southern-hemisphere cuisines around the world. Used to provide a suitable sour flavor in many different kinds of dishes. Available as a plastic wrapped block of pulp, fiber and seeds weighing a few ounces. Choose blocks that are soft and flexible, not hard and dry. Tamarind pulp is used primarily to make Tamarind water.

TAMARIND WATER: Made from store-bought tamarind pulp. Break apart a lump of tamarind pulp about 2 tbsp/30 mL in volume and soak it in a half cup of hot, but not boiling, water. Let stand 10 minutes and strain the mixture before use. Tamarind water will keep for a few days in the fridge and can be frozen for future use.

THAI BASIL: Also known as *bai horabha*, it is reddish purple in color and reminiscent of anise. Used in curries, steamed dishes and soups. Look for Thai basil in Thai, Lao or Vietnamese markets. The Thais use several varieties of basil, *bai krapao* or 'holy basil' having the strongest flavor is actually a type of balsam used in stir-fry dishes. Do not substitute holy basil for Thai basil as its flavor is much too potent.

TOFU: Made from soy bean milk. Tofu is available in a number of consistencies, each degree of firmness used for different types of dishes. I generally use the firm variety at home. Tofu is easily digested and wonderfully nutritious with a slightly nutty flavor when fresh. Make sure you buy it as fresh as possible and use it right away.

TURMERIC: Is a member of the ginger family. The root can be dried and ground into a powder. Its rich yellow color gives curry its characteristic color. Fresh turmeric root can often be found in Thai, Lao or Vietnamese markets. It has a superior flavor to dry powdered turmeric, but be aware that it can easily stain clothing and porous cooking implements. Grind a small piece (½ inch/1 cm long) of the fresh root in place of turmeric powder. You will be surprised by the delicious flavor.

Well, we've reached our final stop and our own personal food safari has come to an end. It has been a great trip and I'm sure we are all going to remember the sights, the sounds and the fabulous flavors.

I said at the beginning that I'd take you out of your kitchen. Well, I hope I did that, but I also hope that you found *Entrée To Asia* entertaining, and that I've helped give you the confidence to go back to your kitchen armed with a little extra knowledge.

So, the next time you're wondering what's for dinner, perhaps you'll try making a little Thai soup or curry, maybe some satay on your barbecue, or a salad with a Southeast Asian twist. I hope so. Don't be afraid to experiment — we're all learning as we go. And remember: don't forget to eat your homework!

Entrée Communications Ltd. takes pleasure in acknowledging the significant financial contribution made by its premiere sponsor ASIAN HOME GOURMET in the production of the television series ENTRÉE TO ASIA on which this cookbook is based.

RECIPES MADE WITH LOVE

For years, food lovers all over the world have turned to Asian Home Gourmet SpicePastes™ to prepare authentic Asian meals. At Asian Home Gourmet, we use only fresh herbs and spices, prepared according to traditional Asian recipes. Unlike other spice pastes, ours are slowly stir-fried to release their essential flavors. No added MSG, preservatives or artificial colorings are added, either.

Continuing our commitment to Asian food, we help bring to you the *Entrée To Asia* television series, hosted by Chef Thomas Robson.

In his unique style, he takes us on a journey through the heart of Asia, exploring local favorites. Inviting us into the kitchen, he prepares some of his own favorite Southeast Asian specialties with equal fanfare.

Happy Cooking!

INDEX OF MAIN INGREDIENTS

ENTRÉE TO ASIA PHOTO CREDITS